RECOLLECTIONS OF
A ROYAL PARISH

Queen Victoria
from an engraving after Sir William Ross R.A. by H.T. Ryall.

Queen Victoria.
from an engraving after Sir William Ross, R.A. by H.T. Ryall.

Walker & Cockerell, ph sc

o

RECOLLECTIONS OF
A ROYAL PARISH

BY PATRICIA LINDSAY

WITH ILLUSTRATIONS

LONDON
JOHN MURRAY, ALBEMARLE STREET
1902

TO

THE HONOURED MEMORY

OF

MY DEAR FATHER

THE MOST OF WHOSE LIFE

WAS SPENT AMID THE SCENES HERE DESCRIBED

THESE PAGES ARE

AFFECTIONATELY DEDICATED

PREFACE

THE following pages do not profess to give a complete picture of Balmoral and its surroundings, still less of the character of our late beloved Queen, or of her life in the Highlands, which has been so vividly portrayed by her own pen. Yet an unskilled hand may sometimes give to a sketch a fresh touch of light or shade, or a dash of local colour, which may be lacking in more finished work.

It has been matter for regret to me that my father* did not leave in writing any record of his early life on Deeside, begun during the second decade of last century, or of the thirty-three years during which he was brought into close connection with the Royal Family, years of devoted attachment and faithful service on his side, and of unvarying kindness, friendship, and consideration on theirs.

* The late Dr. Robertson of Hopewell, Aberdeenshire.

I have had mainly to depend upon my own recollections, aided by the kind help of a few friends who knew the district in the old days, and the small amount of correspondence left among my father's papers.

Now and then in the Highlands, as evening steals on, we see a peak here and there lit up with rosy light, while the valleys are veiled in mist. Like such peaks are the old scenes, events, and faces, which appear in these pages—scattered recollections of the past which stand out most clearly in the sunset light of memory.

PATRICIA LINDSAY.

THE OAKS, BOTLEY, HANTS,
Nov. 8th, 1902.

CONTENTS

CHAPTER I

CRATHIE IN THE OLDEN TIME

CHAPTER II

OLD BALMORAL

CHAPTER III

NEW BALMORAL

LIST OF ILLUSTRATIONS

RECOLLECTIONS OF A ROYAL PARISH

CHAPTER I

CRATHIE IN THE OLDEN TIME

> Let me review the scene
>   And summon from the shadowy past
> The forms that once have been.
>   The Past and Present here unite
> Beneath Time's flowing tide,
>   Like footprints hidden by a brook
> But seen on either side.—LONGFELLOW.

Changes in the Highlands—Life of the people on Deeside early in the last century—Gordons—Farquharsons—Jacobite Risings—"Colonel Anne"—Francis of Monaltrie—Life of the upper classes—Flood of 1829—Shooting tenants—Strathdee, an old hunting ground of the Scottish kings.

IF it be true, as the poet says, that "Time *was* unlocks the riddle of Time *is*," then it may be well that these reminiscences of Crathie should go back a little, to a period beyond my personal recollection, but which is clearly pictured on that page of memory,

B

where are recorded events and habits described to
me in my youth by those of an older generation
who had taken part in them.

The change which the last century has wrought
in the outward and domestic life of the Highlands
is so great as to partake more of the nature of revolution than of that gradual social evolution which
has been universal in other parts of the kingdom.
Nowhere was this change more sudden and more
marked than in Crathie and Braemar, and it may
be said to have dated from about the middle of the
nineteenth century.

Several causes contributed to it; the earliest,
no doubt, the establishment of the penny post and
the wider circulation of newspapers, but still more,
the selection of Balmoral as an autumn residence
for the Court, and the consequent influx of visitors
to Deeside.   This brought money into the country,
with a demand for labour of all kinds at a higher
rate of wages, showing the example and providing
the means of a more luxurious mode of life.

Up to that time Crathie, which with Braemar
formed until 1879 a united parish, though a district
of much natural beauty, was poor, being barren

GENERAL VIEW OF CRATHIE

To face p. 2

in soil and far removed from all large centres of industry. Means of communication were difficult even in summer, and quite impossible in winter, for in the glens the snow lay for many weeks to a depth of several feet. It is on record that at the close of the eighteenth century, in the united parishes of Tullich, Glenmuick, and Glengairn there was only one carriage of any description, but in Crathie the number may have been slightly greater, as there were three resident proprietors.

The crofts, or holdings, seldom exceeded ten to twelve acres, and barely yielded sufficient grain for the support of the family. Agriculture was of the most primitive description : most of the ploughing was done by oxen, and manual labour supplied the rest. The crofters generally possessed a cow, and oatmeal and milk were the staple food of the household. Those who were more well-to-do had a few sheep which they grazed on the hillside, and the wool of these was spun by the women and woven into blankets, plaids, and tartan cloth for the winter clothing of both sexes. Even within my recollection, on the estates of Balmoral, Abergeldie, and Birkhall, comprising in all about thirty thousand acres, only eleven hundred were arable.

These were divided into small farms, or crofts, only two or three exceeding twenty-five acres, and the majority far less, while the number of tenants was over sixty. The crops on these holdings were liable to serious injury from the depredations of deer and other game, for the land was not so well protected by high fences fifty years ago as it is now.

In the beginning of last century the only houses built of stone and lime were those occupied by the lairds, the Manses, and one or two others, including the inns ; hence the name " Stane-house," which in Aberdeenshire is still frequently applied to a country inn. The dwellings of the peasants were mere hovels, built generally of unhewn stones and mud, thatched with heather or broom, and containing two rooms, the "but and ben," divided by wooden partitions and sometimes with a small closet between. The floors—if they could be so called— were of earth, often so uneven that in damp weather pools of water had to be stepped across to reach the peat fire which burned on the hearth.

Coals were an unknown luxury, but on Deeside peat and wood were generally plentiful. Many a good toast have I enjoyed in later years before such a fireplace, with its wide, open chimney, its settle and its "sway," with chain and crook for suspending the big black kettle or three-legged pot. On a cold winter day it was often pleasant to receive the hearty invitation, "Come in by and sit intil the fire and I'll gie ye a bleeze." The "bleeze" consisted generally of fir branches, dried whins (gorse), or "breem cows" (branches of broom).

The only light in the long, dark evenings of winter was derived from one or more small iron lamps of very classic shape, which were fixed on the wall of the cottage, generally by the side of the fireplace. They were called "crusies," and were boat-like in form. The vessels were double, placed one above the other, and train oil was burned in them, with the pith of the rush for wick.

Crusies are rather sought after by collectors on account of their quaint shape, and are now difficult to get, as they have long since given place to the paraffin lamp of modern times.

The windows of these miserable dwellings—often little more than a foot square—were not constructed to open, and afforded but scanty light. It was perhaps as well for health that the walls were draughty, as the supply of fresh air would otherwise have been limited, especially at night, for the family slept in " box beds," shut in by doors carefully closed by day.

At the present time we should consider the conditions of life I have described, as to food and housing, anything but conducive to health, and yet there were few hardier, stronger, and better-grown men than the Highlanders of the last three generations. Probably the pure air and the active outdoor life led by both men and women did much to counteract the unwholesome character of their dwellings.

During the first three or four decades of last century the common wage of a female domestic servant was from £3 to £4 a year, and for a man as groom, gardener, or farm labourer, £10 to £12, exclusive of food. The poor law did not then exist, but the people were thrifty and their wants were few. The fashions in dress preva-

lent in the Lowlands even a century ago were
unknown in the Highlands until many years later.
I have often heard people tell that in their younger
days there was not a bonnet to be seen in the
church of Crathie, except in the lairds' or manse
pews. The old women always wore the picturesque,
high, white muslin "mutch," while the young ones
were bare-headed in summer, save for the ribbon,
or maiden snood, which tied back their hair. The
only mantle was the tartan shawl, which also
served the girls for head-covering when necessary
in winter. Each carried her Bible to church,
generally with a clean pocket-handkerchief folded
round it, and a sprig of thyme or southernwood,
the smelling-bottle of the Highland woman.

When sick or in need the poor people were well
cared for by the proprietors, upon whose land the
ancestors of many of them had lived for several
generations. In fact, the tenantry had descended
in direct lineal succession in the same holdings to
as great an extent as the landlords. Often there
was a distant bond of kinship, or at least of name,
and there was much of the patriarchal in the
relations between them in those old days. These

were far more than a mere business transaction in which neither looked for anything beyond the fulfilment of the stipulations of a lease. The Highlander looked upon his chief as his leader, protector, and almost father. Who does not regret the gradual disappearance of this relic of feudalism ?

The land on the south side of the Dee, from the bridge of Muick to Balmoral, was formerly owned by the lairds of Abergeldie, and most of their tenants bore the name of Gordon. The Gordons were not of Highland origin, and it is curious to note that in the early part of last century the use of the Gaelic language had almost died out on their property; while on the north bank of the Dee, of which the Farquharsons—a Celtic family—were proprietors, the old tongue still held sway. In my childhood Gaelic was very generally spoken in Braemar, but only by a few old people in Crathie, though many understood, and probably could speak it if occasion required.

Parish schools were an old institution in Scotland at the time of which I write, and education, though not what it afterwards became, was even then fairly good in Upper Deeside, but owing to the severity of the winter climate and the distance in many cases from school, attendance was very irregular, and numbers of the poorer people were unable to write, and some even to read.

From all I have heard, however, I think the people of the early part of last century would in the essentials of a good moral life compare favourably with their descendants, over whom the Church exercises less rigorous discipline, but whose advantages in many ways are so much greater. Every age has its special vices, and in Crathie poaching and smuggling belonged to that time. The first is now rare, and the second has ceased entirely, though I fear the consumption of whisky has not greatly diminished among the working classes. The remote glens of the Highlands seem to lend themselves temptingly to a safe indulgence in illicit distilling, but in the old times it was by no means confined to them and was sometimes carried on in unlikely places.

The Farquharsons, who formerly shared with the Gordons the possession of all the land in Crathie and Braemar, came originally from Rothiemurchus,

and not later than towards the close of the
fifteenth century, for we know that the grandson of
the first Farquharson who settled on Deeside fell
carrying the Royal Standard at the Battle of
Pinkie. They found Gordons already in possession near Braemar, for it is recorded that a certain
Donald Farquharson fancied the lands of Invercauld, where a Gordon had fixed his residence.
These were the days of

> "The simple plan
> That they should take who have the power,
> And they should keep who can."

So Gordon, it is to be feared, had summary and
forcible notice to quit. The families seem afterwards, however, to have settled their differences,
for they intermarried on two or three occasions.

The Farquharsons took a prominent part in the
wars of the seventeenth and eighteenth centuries,
and always on the Jacobite side until 1745, when
a little skilful hedging took place between two
branches of the family. Invercauld remained true
to the Hanoverian succession, while Monaltrie and
others joined Prince Charlie, thus making the
Farquharsons fairly safe in any eventuality.

In the beginning of 1745 three companies of
militia were raised, mainly in the Aberdeenshire
and Perthshire Highlands, as a reserve for the
old "Black Watch," then serving abroad. James
Farquharson, younger of Invercauld, and his
brother-in-law, the laird of Mackintosh, both held
commissions in this corps, and were thus in the pay
of the Government. Lady Mackintosh's sympathies,
however, were quite on the other side, and in the
absence of her husband and brother she raised the
Clan Mackintosh and as many of the Farquharsons
as she could influence, and did good service for the
cause of the Prince, earning for herself the title of
"Colonel Anne."

The allegiance of the militia was but half-hearted;
some refused to leave their native county as contrary
to the agreement under which they enlisted, and
many deserted on the eve of the Battle of Preston-
pans. Some even of the officers contrived to have
themselves taken prisoners by their own clansmen,
and the sequel to the story of the laird of Mackintosh and his military wife is so curious that I may
be excused for giving it here. I quote from *Deeside
Tales*, by the Rev. John Michie, of Dinnet.

"This brave officer," the laird of Mackintosh, "on being apprehended by a party of Highland scouts, demanded to be brought before a person of rank to whom he might surrender himself a prisoner of war. He was accordingly conducted into the presence of his wife, then acting the part of chief of the clan in the Chevalier's army. As he presented his sword she greeted him in true military style, 'Your servant, Captain,' to which he replied with equal brevity, 'your servant, Colonel,' and so they ended the matter."

It is said that five hundred Farquharsons joined the standard of Prince Charlie, but it is doubtful whether the number was so large. The laird of Invercauld and his people had suffered so much in 1715 that he did all in his power to discourage the rising, and there are documents extant which go to prove that there was little eagerness on the part of the clansmen again to don the white cockade. Far-quharson of Balmoral, who had been out in 1715 as A.D.C. to the Earl of Mar, was the first of the clan to take up arms for the Prince in '45. He was severely wounded at the Battle of Falkirk, and then the command of the Farquharsons devolved upon

Francis of Monaltrie. After the disastrous defeat of Culloden Francis was taken prisoner, conveyed to London, and there tried and condemned to death. On the eve of his execution, or some say on the very morning of the day, he was reprieved from the death penalty, though not pardoned. There is a romantic story that this leniency was obtained through the influence of a lady of rank whose heart was touched by the good looks, as well as the misfortunes, of the Highland chief. There may be some truth in the story, as Francis Farquharson, the "Baron Ban" (*i.e.* fair-haired), as he was called, was reputed to be the handsomest man in the Prince's army; but on the other hand, similar grace was shown to a few more of the same batch of prisoners, one—also a Farquharson—being reprieved after he had been placed in the cart for conveyance to Tyburn. The little romance remains, therefore, neither proved nor refuted. For twenty years Francis Farquharson was forbidden to go further north than Hertfordshire, but eventually on the payment of a certain sum, the attainder was removed from his estates, and he was allowed to return to Deeside. His nephew, an old friend of my father's, was the last laird of Monaltrie, which is now merged in the Invercauld property. He was a Whig in politics, and used to tell the story of a little passage of arms between himself and the poet Burns at a public banquet in Edinburgh. Mr. Farquharson had alluded to the part played by his uncle in the rebellion of 1745, and in a subsequent speech the poet, who was a strong Jacobite, remarked that " Mr. Farquharson had no reason to be ashamed of his ancestors, whatever reason they might have to be ashamed of him."

The divisions caused in families and districts by Jacobite and anti-Jacobite feeling often led to curious scenes. One such occurred in a parish, not exactly neighbouring to Crathie, but in the same presbytery. Charles Gordon of Blelack was a colonel in the Prince's army, while the minister of Logie Coldstone, in whose parish Blelack is situated, was presumably on the other side, or at least felt in duty bound to pray for the success of the Government forces.

During the service in church one Sunday, while the rebellion was in progress, he besought the Almighty to scatter the army of the rebels, and bring their counsels to nought. Unfortunately the mother of Colonel Gordon was present, and, standing up in her pew, the lady of Blelack, with an oath, demanded, "How daur ye say that and my Charlie wi' them!"

When my father first came to Deeside in 1818, there was only one other doctor within fifty miles, so it may be imagined that the circuit of his practice was a wide one, and for many years his work was entirely done on horseback. In fact, over a great part of the Highlands any other means of locomotion would in those days have been impossible, and many a time he has told me of riding forty miles to the borders of Banffshire and Inverness-shire before breakfast. He was an excellent horseman, and rode with lightness and ease till past eighty years of age.

An event that occurred during his residence at Crathie, of which I have often heard him speak, was the great flood of 1829, which left its mark upon the physical features of the country as well as upon the minds of the inhabitants. Large pieces of land became dislodged, and with bridges, houses, furniture, crops and animals were swept into one wild, confused mass of ruin and carried down the raging torrent. The house my father occupied was close to the junction of a rapid mountain stream with the Dee, and for many hours was in imminent danger of being undermined. Water was standing to the depth of some feet on the ground floor, and I remember his saying that after it subsided, a fish was found caught in the plate-rack in the kitchen.

One trace of the '45 rebellion still remained when my father came to Crathie, in the company of soldiers stationed at Mar Castle to ensure the peace of the Highlands. I do not think that in his time they were ever called upon to exercise their martial authority, and in a few years they were removed; but while there the officers made a pleasant addition to the rather limited society of the district.

Besides the Farquharsons and Gordons, the Earls of Fife owned a considerable amount of land in the neighbourhood of Braemar, though compared with the other two families they were new-comers on Deeside. It was, I think, in 1737 that Lord Braco, the ancestor of the present Duke of Fife, bought the estate of Farquharson of

Allanquoich, and to this, in 1798, was added Balmoral. During my father's early residence on Deeside the grand-uncle of the present peer held the title and lands. He was somewhat eccentric and led the life of a recluse, but to those he liked he was both kind and hospitable.

Invercauld was then in the hands of a lady who was married to a Ross of Balnagowan, but held the Farquharson property in her own right; and a very important person on Deeside was "the leddy of Invercauld," as she was always styled by the country folks.

The proprietors of those days exercised a kindly hospitality, more simple and homely than in the present day, but not the less enjoyable on that account. The landowners lived more on their Scottish estates; their residences were not merely occupied for three or four months of a shooting season, they were real family homes. Some went to Aberdeen, some to Edinburgh for part of the winter, travelling in the family coach, but for the greater portion of the year they resided in the Highlands, and except by the nobility a London season was not thought of.

C

In few things has there been a greater change within the last sixty or seventy years, than in the housekeeping of a Highland establishment. Butchers and bakers were then unknown. Even within my recollection the baker from Ballater only visited Crathie once a week, and the butcher not at all. Very little wheat flour was used even in moderately large houses, and all baking was done at home. The bread of the poorer people was oatcakes and barley-meal scones only. The Dee supplied salmon and trout for the greater part of the year, so the fishmonger could be dispensed with; and as to meat, there was always abundance of excellent hill-fed mutton, and chickens at 6*d.* apiece from the cottagers if the home-supply ran short. Rent was often partly paid in kind, so there was sometimes rather a superfluity of poultry. Game, including red and roe deer venison, was always plentiful in the season, and often in a severe winter I have had excellent grouse which had been in the larder five or six weeks after the close of the shooting. In the early part of the winter most households of any size killed what was called a " mart," that is, a well-fed young ox, so named from the season of Martinmas, about which time it was usually killed. As much of the beef as would keep good was left fresh for immediate consumption, and the rest salted for winter use. Sometimes two neighbouring families would share a mart between them, and I have heard that occasionally relatives and intimate friends used to adjourn to each other's houses in turn during the winter, and remain till the respective marts were consumed.

The killing of the mart was still a regular custom in my childhood, and I can now recall what a busy time it was in the household. With what interest we young ones watched the preparations for pickling, making of white and black puddings, potted head, etc., etc., while the conversion of tallow into mould, or dip candles, was quite a fascinating spectacle; but how thankful we may be that they are now only "a light of other days"!

Various shooting tenants added much to the social cheerfulness of the autumn on Deeside even in the early part of last century. Among them were one or two Waterloo veterans, and Sir David Baird, the hero of Seringapatam, of whom an appreciative mother said when she heard of his being a prisoner and chained to a soldier, " Lord help the man that's chained to oor Davie! "

A romantic story attached to one sportsman lives in my memory. A gentleman of large property in England fell a victim to the charms of a Highland lass, handsome Nellie Coutts, whom he sent to an English school to be educated, and then married, taking her abroad afterwards for a year or two of foreign travel. She had been the friend and fellow-servant of my father's cook, and some time after her marriage she and her husband were again in Aberdeenshire and dined with my father. I have often heard him say he hardly recognised Nellie Coutts in the handsome, dignified lady who sat on his right hand, and even in her speech had hardly a touch of the mountain tongue. To her credit be it said she made an opportunity in the course of the evening to have a long, homely chat over old times with her former companion, who was still in my father's service. The marriage was a happy but childless one, and Nellie was rather early left a rich widow, who bestowed her wealth mainly upon the Roman Catholic Church, of which she was a member.

The abundance of game in Crathie and Braemar made the old Castle of Kindrochit (Mar Castle) a favourite hunting-seat of the early kings of Scotland and their nobles, and in an old charter of 1564 we find Queen Mary conveying the lands and lordship of Braemar and Strathdee, which included Balmoral, to James, Earl of Moray. It does not appear, however, that the Earls of Moray long kept possession of Balmoral, for it passed into the hands of the Farquharsons early in the following century.

It seems strange that after the lapse of nearly three hundred years the feet of another Sovereign should have been drawn to the same district, and that, in spite of the many and varied attractions of other places, Crathie should still have had the same charm for Queen Victoria as for the Scottish monarchs of old, and so earn for a second time in its history the title of a Royal Parish.

CHAPTER II

OLD BALMORAL

" The Mavis still doth sweetly sing,
    The bluebells sweetly blaw,
The bonny Dee's* clear winding still,
    But 'the Auld House' is awa."—LADY NAIRNE.

IN writing of Crathie it is inevitable that the first place should be given to Balmoral as the centre of most general interest.

The natural features of its surroundings are too well known to need further description, for photographs, sketches, and books have made the upper valley of the Dee, with its rugged hills and lovely woods of self-sown birch and pine, familiar even to those who have not gazed upon its beauty for

* *Earn* in the original song.

22

themselves. An ideal home of healthful rest it seems, where "the mountains speak peace" to those who are weary of crowds and ceremony, or the burden of State cares.

The derivation of the name "Balmoral" has been the subject of much discussion among Gaelic scholars. It is undoubtedly Celtic, and the first syllable " Bal," from " baile," a town, is undisputed, the word "town" or "toun" being constantly applied in Scotland to a single farmhouse and offices.

It is over the second part, "moral," that debates have arisen. Into these I need not enter here, for the bulk of skilled opinion is in favour of the derivation from the adjective "morail," meaning great or stately. The situation is undoubtedly fine, and possibly the buildings, viewed with regard to the time and the remoteness of the locality, may have been considerable. Hence the name "Great-toun" might well be appropriate. My father had a theory that Balmoral owed its name to the lime quarries in the vicinity. Thus, " Bal" (town, farm, or homestead), "mor" (large, abundant), "aol" (lime, limestone, or chalk). He did not profess to be proficient in the language, and whether his derivation met with support from any Gaelic scholars I cannot say.

Balmoral was originally the property of the Farquharsons of Inverey, and was bought from them by the second Earl of Fife about the close of the eighteenth century.

I do not think any of the Duff family ever lived there, and after my father came to Deeside, in 1818, it was occupied for some years by a Captain Cameron and his family, who were followed by various shooting tenants.

Balmoral was a familiar name to me from my earliest childhood, and was at that time rented by Sir Robert Gordon, brother to the Earl of Aberdeen, who was Premier of the Coalition Cabinet at the time of the Crimean War. Sir Robert had been British Ambassador at Vienna, and was a man of sterling worth, ability, and kindness, loved and respected by all who knew him. He added largely to the Castle, and made it a centre of hospitality to the country for many miles around. Sir Robert's sister, Lady Alicia Gordon, was much with him at Balmoral, and was a kind and popular hostess. Tales of these Balmoral festivities, heard from my father and mother, and drunk in eagerly by childish ears, linger yet in my recollection ; the dates are hazy, but all belong to Sir Robert's time —a tenancy extending over several years, I think.

There were two ladies of whose beauty I heard much : one—the venerable Duchess of Abercorn— still survives at upwards of ninety, with about one hundred and fifty living descendants around her. She was a very graceful dancer in her youth, and I have often heard my father speak of one occasion when she and another lady whose name I forget donned short skirts and danced "Gille Calum," to the intense admiration of the company. The mother of the Duchess of Abercorn was a well - known figure on Deeside, the eccentric Duchess of Bedford, of whom many tales were still told in Crathie in my young days. She was a daughter of the celebrated Jane, Duchess of Gordon, whom in many ways, especially freedom of speech, she greatly resembled. She was a keen sportswoman, and tramped the heather like a man. An old Highland servant of ours used to tell me, apropos of the old Scottish custom—now happily obsolete—of a man saluting his partner with a kiss

before commencing a reel, that the Duchess of
Bedford, having selected her partner and taken her
place in the dance, used to say, " Now, Campbell,
be sure you begin in the correct fashion," or, after
he had made his bow and commenced to dance,
would call him back and say, " You have forgotten
something, my man." Of course, it was only done
to teaze and enjoy the confusion her words caused,
for woe be to the partner who presumed on the
invitation! But it reminds one of the well-known
story of her mother, the Duchess of Gordon, who
tried to puzzle George IV. with the Scottish
sentence, "Come prie my mou, my canty callant."

The other beauty was Miss Lane Fox, who died
young and unmarried. She was a niece of the
Duke and Duchess of Leeds, who occupied Old
Mar Lodge for many years, and gathered there
a lively circle of artistic and sporting guests. In
those days, when ladies did not go in so much for
shooting and fishing as many do now, Mrs. Horatio
Ross was rather a celebrity on Deeside. Deer-
stalking was her favourite pastime, and she was
a splendid markswoman. Her husband, too, was
a crack shot, and the skill of the parents descended

to their sons, one of whom was the champion rifle-
shot in the early days of the Wimbledon Meeting.

Game was very plentiful in Crathie and Braemar
in the middle of the last century, and I think it was
at Mar Lodge that a petition was sent in by the
servants that they might not have salmon or
venison more than twice a week! The rents then
given for shooting and fishing, when the sport was
better, would now be considered absurdly low.
Within my recollection my father paid £10 a year
for fishing on the Dee, which now brings from
£150 to £200.

Sir Edwin Landseer was a frequent visitor at
Mar Lodge and Balmoral, and there made many
studies for some of his best-known pictures.

I well remember Sir Robert Gordon's sudden
death, which occurred while sitting at the break-
fast-table, in the autumn of 1847. My father was
to have been his guest that morning at Balmoral,
but was detained, and arrived an hour late to find
that his friend had passed away. Though a very
little child at that time, I can recall now the grief
which his death caused in our household, as well
as the trivial incident of clambering up to the high

sill of an attic window to see the plumed hearse
which conveyed his body pass our approach gate
on its way to Haddo House for interment. I have
no recollection of ever seeing Sir Robert Gordon,
but Lord Aberdeen was a familiar figure to me in
my early youth, for he survived his brother many
years. He was a tall, thin man, with a long face
and grave aspect, rather awe-inspiring to a child,
and perhaps this feeling was heightened by the
reverence with which my father regarded him. He
considered him one of the best and most reliable
of men, thoroughly kind in a quiet, undemonstrative
way ; but what impressed me most was his perfect
confidence in his lordship's justice : whatever he
said or did was accepted by my father as true, fair
and right.

"The Gordons" are so popular in these days
that perhaps I may be pardoned for making a
digression down the Dee from Crathie for a little,
and describing another "gallant Gordon" who was
a very vivid personality to my childhood—the
old Marquis of Huntly, grandfather of the present
peer, and then head of the clan, the dukedom of
Gordon being extinct. He was a frequent guest

at my father's, and I can see the sharp, eager, old
face now, as he sat at the whist-table—for he was
a keen whist player—and in right of his age and
rank allowed to revoke with impunity.

He was an old beau of the Regency, carefully
dressed to the last, and a good deal "made up,"
the blue-blackness of his hair—or wig—impressing
me very much. He was a small, thin man, with
very courtly manners, popular with everybody, and
very kind to us children. I remember so well his
telling me of having danced a minuet at Versailles
with Marie Antoinette, and the thrill it sent through
me to be thus brought, as it seemed, almost into
touch with the tragedy of the French Revolution.
The beautiful queen was the favourite heroine of
my childhood, and this much-to-be-envied experience
of Lord Huntly's shed a halo of romance over
him also.

In 1848, the year following the death of Sir
Robert Gordon, a Highland residence was wanted
for the Queen, and Sir James Clark, her physician,
strongly recommended Deeside, of the pure bracing
air of which he had the highest opinion. Balmoral,
being vacant, was suggested and accepted; and in

September, 1848, commenced that long series of
visits to Deeside which were only broken by the
lamented death of the Queen.

Memory brings clearly before me the bright
autumn day when my sister and I were taken by
some of our elders to a point of the road between
Aboyne and Ballater to have our first sight of
Royalty. The first coming of the Queen created
a great excitement in the quiet countryside, which
had never dreamed of being so favoured ; the
people collected in crowds in all the villages along
the route from Aberdeen to Balmoral—for there
were no railways in those days—and triumphal
arches and flags were everywhere. It was but a
passing glimpse we got of a lady and gentleman
with two children in an open carriage, who bowed
and smiled in response to the respectful salutations
of our little group.

The children were the late Empress of Germany
and our present gracious King ; they were of much
the same age as my sister and myself, and were
therefore of special interest to us from some lingering expectation that we might not find them cast
in quite the same mould as children of lower

degree. I can hardly tell now how far my impressions of the royal party are founded upon my own childish observation or the remarks of those around me, but a vivid picture remains on my mental vision of a strikingly handsome man, and beside him a bright face, framed in a simple straw bonnet, with a keen glance which seemed to take note of everything. Royal Stewart tartan was conspicuous in the draperies of the carriage, as it afterwards was in the furnishing of the new castle at Balmoral, for the Queen's heart was ever "warm to the tartan."

My father was not with us, having been asked by Lord Aberdeen to make all arrangements at Balmoral for the reception of the Queen and Prince Consort, and to meet them on arrival. These arrangements were so satisfactory, and the royal pair so favourably impressed by my father personally, that backed as he was by the warm recommendation of Lord Aberdeen — always a trusted counsellor of his Sovereign in affairs great and small—this introduction led to his appointment as Commissioner in Scotland for the Queen, the Prince Consort, and later for the Prince of Wales, a combined post which he held for nearly thirty years.

Her Majesty has herself given to the world her first impressions of Balmoral, and told how year by year the place and people wound themselves more and more closely round her heart.

The old castle was a picturesque building, with a battlemented tower, and harmonised well with its surroundings, but its accommodation was unsuited to the requirements of a royal retinue, and, when the lease of Balmoral was taken over by the Prince Consort from the representatives of Sir Robert Gordon, large additions at the back, principally for the use of servants, were at once commenced.

I have spent many happy days in the old house at Balmoral, playing with the children of the old steward, François d'Albertanson, who had been major-domo to Sir Robert Gordon and, with his wife, who acted for some years as housekeeper, was retained in the Queen's service until both died. François was a most amusing and excitable old Frenchman, with an intense hatred of the Bonapartes. Nothing roused him so much as to tell him

THE OLD CASTLE OF BALMORAL

To face p. 32

it was rumoured that the Emperor Napoleon III.
was to pay the Queen a visit at Balmoral; he
would then, to the delight of his youthful audience,
utter the most ferocious threats and dance with
rage. These little ebullitions of French vivacity
were quite harmless, and had His Imperial Majesty
ever come to Balmoral, he would have been perfectly
safe. The grounds were at this time overrun with
rabbits, and I shall never forget the exciting delights
of hunting them with ferrets and Sir Robert's old
dog, Monkey, one of the most sagacious of animals.
As far as my knowledge of dogs goes, he was of a
nondescript breed, more resembling an overgrown
Skye terrier than anything else, but he had the
brains which are sometimes the compensation of
mongrels. He was a great favourite with the
Queen, who speaks of him as "Monk" in her
Journal.

I think it must have been in the following year
—1849—that I next remember seeing the Queen,
and it was in Crathie Church. She and the Prince
Consort, with the two ladies in attendance, sat in
the Balmoral pew in the front of the gallery, and
the equerries and other gentlemen of the Court

D

in the seat immediately behind. Of the service
I remember nothing; the two things which impressed me most were the beauty of the Duchess
of Wellington, then Marchioness of Douro, and
lady-in-waiting at the time, and the disappointment
I felt at the absence of the royal children. While
very young they never attended the Presbyterian
Church, and I think the rule was that they
should not do so until after their confirmation.
The Queen and Prince were both accomplished
musicians, and took a great interest in the
psalmody of Crathie Church, encouraging the
teaching of singing in the schools of the district
and in every way trying to improve this part of
the service, with most successful results.

My recollection of the Prince Consort at this
time is of a tall, handsome man, still slight, and
holding himself very upright, and with a calm,
thoughtful expression of countenance. I had few
opportunities of meeting him after I attained an
age when my impressions would be of any value,
but I remember that, while ever gentle and
courteous, he had a reserved manner apt to be
mistaken for hauteur by strangers. He had little

" small talk," but I have seen him converse with great eagerness and animation, and his face light up with keen interest and often with quiet humour when discussing a congenial topic. Though active and a thorough sportsman, the Prince was never a strong man, and very dependent upon regular nourishment. I have often heard my father, after being out on the hills with His Royal Highness, bewail his ready fatigue and small reserve of strength. Consequently when the news of his illness reached us in 1861, and long before any danger was hinted at, this lack of vitality made my father from the first intensely anxious as to the result of the fever.

Like all who had the privilege of much intercourse with him, my father was devoted to the Prince, and often spoke of him as the finest character he had ever known ; so many-sided and gifted, clear-sighted and quick in his comprehension of business details, and in his judgment of the men he had to deal with ; ever guided by the highest religious principle, and showing wisdom beyond his years, for he was still a young man— under thirty—when he first came to Deeside.

Balmoral was purchased by the Prince Consort

from the trustees of the Earl of Fife in 1852. His Royal Highness bequeathed it to the Queen at his death, and she, in turn, arranged that thereafter it should be the property of the reigning Sovereign. Soon after the purchase of the estate the new castle was commenced, and I can recall now the interest with which I watched the progress of the building from time to time. The foundation stone was laid in September, 1853, and in 1855 the portion finished was occupied by the Royal Family; but some members of the suite and most of the servants were still under the old roof. It was not until the autumn of 1856 that the whole was completed and the Balmoral of my childhood swept away.

CHAPTER III

NEW BALMORAL

"Know'st thou the land of the mountain and flood,
   Where the pines of the forest for ages have stood ;
   Where the eagles come forth on the wings of the storm,
   And their young ones are rocked on the high Cairngorm ? "

THE granite of which the new castle is built was
quarried on the estate ; the grain of the stone is

very fine, and it is unusually white, the felspar
which generally supplies the colouring matter in
granite being in this case nearly colourless. The
late Sir Charles Lyell, the eminent geologist, in an
interesting letter to my father upon the geological
features of the Balmoral property, says that the
granite is pure quartz, felspar and mica, without
any calcareous matter, though there are beds of
limestone in the immediate neighbourhood. At a
distance the effect of the building is like white
marble, but a nearer view shows the crystalline
sparkle which imparts such beauty to granite.
There has been of late years a wonderful develop-
ment in the dressing and carving of granite, but at
the time Balmoral was built it was considered a
wonderful specimen of workmanship in such a hard
material.

The style is Scottish Baronial, and Mr. William
Smith of Aberdeen was the architect; but many
suggestions and alterations were made by the
Prince Consort. The decoration and furnishing of
the interior were severely simple; objects of the
chase, and Highland trophies and weapons, with
engravings from Landseer, were the main adorn-

BALMORAL CASTLE AND LOCHNAGAR

To face p. 38

ment of the walls; royal and hunting Stewart tartan formed the design of most of the carpets and curtains, and the whole woodwork of the house was of pitch-pine varnished. The Prince Consort was specially anxious that everything should be in keeping with the locality, and the fact was insisted on that this was no palace, but simply a royal shooting-box in the Highlands. There were to be no valuable oil-paintings and no lavish decoration, only comfort and harmony were to be considered.

The site of the new castle is nearer the river than its predecessor, and a little further from the base of the beautiful birch-clothed hill of Craig-Gowan; it commands a more uninterrupted view towards the west, which is the aspect of nearly all the rooms occupied by the Queen and Prince Consort. The grounds were entirely laid out according to his plans, and under his direction. To the last, Balmoral was to the Queen a memorial of her beloved husband, and she always spoke of the place as "his own creation, own work, own building, own laying out," with "the impress of his dear hand stamped everywhere."

In a work upon *The Prince Consort's Farms*, by
J. C. Morton, to which my father contributed the
chapter upon Balmoral, he thus writes of His Royal
Highness and his efforts on behalf of the Highland
people around him :—

To increase the comforts of his tenants and to elevate
their moral and social condition were objects steadily kept
in view from the time the Prince became a proprietor of
Highland property, and they were pursued with unabated
zeal till the end of his life. Schools were erected and
teachers appointed for the education of the young, and to
give a taste for reading and increase the means of information an excellent library, the joint gift of H.M. the Queen
and the Prince, was established at Balmoral and thrown
open, not only to tenants and servants, but to all in the
neighbourhood. . . . Comfortable cottages have replaced
the former miserable dwellings ; farm offices, according to
the size of the farms, have been erected ; money has been
advanced for the draining, trenching, and improvement of
waste land ; new roads have been opened up and old ones
repaired ; fences have been renewed and upwards of one
thousand acres of unreclaimable land planted. But it was
not to agricultural improvements alone that His Royal
Highness's attention was directed ; he saw the advantage
of encouraging tradesmen and labourers of good character
to settle upon his estates. Houses and gardens, with a
croft where it could be conveniently added, were provided

at a moderate rent, and the extensive works thus under-taken were carried on over a series of years so as to give constant employment.

The touching story of the happy, but all too brief domestic country life led by the Queen and Prince at Balmoral, with its walks and drives, its sport and longer excursions—taken incognito, when they thoroughly enjoyed the mystification they caused to the good people of the villages and inns where they rested—has been told by the Queen herself, and needs not an added word from me.

Three occasions prior to the death of the Prince Consort when I had the honour of meeting him, as well as the Queen and various members of the Royal Family, stand out more prominently than any others in my memory. In 1857 the Queen and Prince Consort, with their four elder children, honoured my father and mother with a visit at Indego, on their way to Haddo House. Her Majesty's gracious motherliness impressed me much that day—she took such kindly notice of some little grandsons of my father's who were with us; one, a very pretty boy, she specially admired and kissed warmly, a caress of which he was proud to his dying day. The

Prince Consort was much interested in agricultural matters, and I remember well his appreciative inspection of my father's farm, stock of polled cattle, etc.

The visit was at the close of their autumn stay on Deeside, and it was the Princess Royal's last sojourn at Balmoral before her marriage. Two years had elapsed since the September day on Craig-na-Ban, when by means of a piece of white heather, supposed in flower language to imply a declaration of love, that modern Arthur, the brave, noble-hearted Emperor Frederick of Germany, told once more "the old story," and won the promise of our gifted Princess Royal to be his wife. One who knew him well* has compared the silent tragedy of his death to the "passing of Arthur," and certainly in courage, chivalry, and goodness he was kin in spirit to Tennyson's stainless king.

I remember well the Princess's tearful face that day at Indego, for, though full of love and hope, she was sad at bidding farewell to the Highland home which was so dear to her. She always seemed to me very unlike her brothers and sisters in appear-

* The Right Hon. Sir Edward Malet, G.C.B., G.C.M.G.

ance : the type of face was different, and though not handsome in feature was highly intelligent, and in youth very winning. I did not see her again until the shadow of the great sorrow of her life was already resting upon her and leaving its impress on the careworn, anxious face. She was a woman of high intellectual power, inheriting, in the Queen's opinion, much of her father's nature and talent.

Of Princess Alice I remember little at this time, except her sweet, beautiful face, but in after life— looked at quite apart from her high rank—she dwells in my recollection as one of the most attractive women I ever met. In this Princess womanliness and dignity were perfectly combined, and with them a kindly frankness that was very charming. She visited my father and me, with the Grand Duke and two of her children, shortly after the conclusion of the Franco-German War—to her a time of sore anxiety and unsparing beneficent labour ; and the wifely pride in her brave soldier husband, and thankfulness for his safe return, expressed in such a natural, womanly way in her conversation, touched and impressed me deeply.

The tower of strength and comfort which, though quite a girl, she proved to our widowed Queen is known to all. To herself the loss of her father was a lifelong grief, and his teaching and example were as a lamp to her often difficult path until, on the seventeenth anniversary of his death, she joined him "within the veil."

The following touching autograph letter from Her Majesty was received by my father in answer to his expression of deep sorrow and respectful sympathy on the occasion of the death of the Grand Duchess of Hesse.

"OSBORNE, *January 8th*, 1879.

The Queen must write at once to thank Dr. Robertson for his very kind letter, and all his expressions of true sympathy in the terrible loss she and her family have just sustained. Dr. Robertson knew her darling child from her sixth year, and saw her grow up all that fondest parents could desire, and can therefore understand our grief at her early removal from this world. But in the midst of her overwhelming grief, for the loss of such a daughter, wife and mother, it is gratifying and soothing to her, as well as to the broken-hearted Grand-Duke and all her brothers and sisters, to see how universal the sympathy is, and how much she was beloved for her noble, courageous, gentle and self-sacrificing character.

It is difficult for us to understand why, as in 1861, a life so valuable and so necessary should be taken away. But we know that what God does is right, and we can only submit and strive to say " Thy will be done," as Dr. Robertson so justly observes.

The Queen has not actually suffered in health, but she feels shaken and depressed.

She expects her poor son-in-law with his dear children here in a fortnight.

She encloses a photograph of dear Alice for Dr. Robertson.

In 1859 His Royal Highness the Prince Consort was President of the British Association, which held its Annual Meeting that year in Aberdeen, and the address which he delivered at the opening ceremony excited the warm admiration of all who heard it. A fête was given at Balmoral for the members of the Association, and Highland games were arranged for their amusement at the west side of the castle, beyond the terraced garden. I remember the gay and picturesque scene well, and also the bitterly cold showery weather which sadly marred the pleasure of the day. Nearly all the residents on Deeside were collected there, besides

the *savants* and their attendant multitude of admiring followers.   The Farquharson, Duff, and Forbes
Highlanders, headed by their respective chiefs,
marched to the ground with pipes playing and
plaids waving in the wind.   The Royal Family,
bright in Stewart tartan, occupied the terrace over-
looking the games, and were semicircled by the
savants, the suite, and invited guests.   Those
leading members of the Association privileged to
occupy this position formed an interesting group,
among them many names still standing high in the
ranks of science, though those who bore them are
no longer with us : Professor Owen, Sir Roderick
Murchison, Sir David Brewster, Sir John Bowring,
and many others.

In such a company the Prince Consort was in
his element, his wide general culture enabling him
to converse with each intelligently and apprecia-
tively on his own special subject.   The usual order
of Highland competitions was followed — tossing
the caber, throwing the hammer, putting the stone,
racing, dancing, etc.—and prizes were bestowed by
the Queen and Prince, who remained on the ground
till dusk, when all dispersed.   Refreshments were

Walker &Cockerell, ph. sc.

The Prince Consort
From a photograph by C. Silvy.

served in the ballroom, and I shall never forget
the crush of the hungry crowd. The scientific mind
I there learned was not indifferent to the claims of
the material tabernacle.

The following year—1860—I was present at a
ball at Balmoral, what the country people used to
call "a quality ball," and the last of the kind I
believe that was ever given there.   In 1861 the
Court was in mourning for H.R.H. the Duchess
of Kent, and ere the year closed the blow fell
which shadowed the whole of the Queen's after-
life.

Many things make that evening a marked occasion to me and one I shall never forget. It was my
first ball after I was grown up, and I thoroughly
enjoyed it both as a spectacle and a social festivity.
My first partner was a very juvenile one, the
present Duke of Fife, then Lord Macduff.   He
was marching about the room in full Highland
dress, in a very independent way for such a small
boy, and after stopping to survey critically the
group of ladies near me, came up in a straightforward childish fashion and put out his hand,
saying, "Will you dance with me?"   As far as I

can tell he did not even know my name, but at his age an introduction was hardly necessary.

The Queen and Prince Consort both took part in the dancing, as well as the younger members of the Royal Family who were present. In those days Her Majesty was still a light and spirited dancer of Scotch reels, which with quadrilles and country dances formed the greater part of the programme. There may have been one or two valses and polkas, but, if so, they were very few.

In after years many dances of a mixed character were given at Balmoral, principally for the tenants and servants, but often including those of higher rank resident in the neighbourhood. The Queen always enjoyed seeing her people happy, and encouraged the keeping up of all old Highland customs, such as the torchlight dance of the keepers and ghillies when the stags were brought home after a good day's stalking. Weirdly picturesque scenes these dances were, held in front of the castle, with the hills and woods and the figures of the men fitfully lit up by the light of the blazing pine torches. The old customs belonging to Hallowe'en always interested the Queen, and she desired that they should be fully carried out when she was at Balmoral. Consequently bonfires blazed on many of the hills, and lighted torches, called "sownachs," were borne round the bounds of the various farms and homesteads to keep off the evil spirits supposed to be let loose on All Hallow's Eve. The effect was extremely pretty when from some elevated point of view numbers of these torches could be seen flitting about the valley, while the fires were burning on the heights.

When Her Majesty was at Balmoral a Cabinet Minister was always in attendance, and as they took it in turn for varying periods of time, three or four members of the Government were generally to be seen there in the course of the season. My father came into contact, more or less intimately, with many men who have left their mark on the history of our time, and with some of them, such as Sir George Grey, Mr. W. E. Forster, and others, he formed a warm friendship. Of Lord Beaconsfield, Mr. Gladstone, Lord Granville, and, in earlier days, Earl Russell and Lord Palmerston, he often spoke. Lord Granville he found genial

E

and kindly, quite the courtier and a *persona grata* with all.

To Lord Beaconsfield, though admiring him warmly as a politician, my father was not much drawn. Disraeli, too, had a touch of the courtier, and was very fond of ladies' society, in which he made himself very agreeable, but to most gentlemen he was very reserved and wanting in the *bonhomie* which made Lord Granville so popular. At times, however, his "table-talk" was brilliant and very satirical.

Apart from politics—which they never discussed —my father had a great admiration for Mr. Gladstone, whose vast information on all subjects and wonderful conversational powers he greatly enjoyed. They often walked together when Mr. Gladstone was at Balmoral, and a more interesting companion, he often said, it would be hard to find; his knowledge of all kinds of literature, even purely local, such as legends and ballads, being most unusual.

Earl Russell and his family occupied Abergeldie Castle for one or two seasons, and he was therefore well known on Deeside. He was a shabby-looking little man, quite indifferent to dress and personal appearance, but when he was understood and his peculiarities got over, he was respected and liked.

My father often told the story of an awkward position in which he was once placed by Lord Palmerston. The popular Lord Pam, as is clearly brought out in the *Life of the Prince Consort*, was often rather troublesome to his Sovereign in affairs of State, and even to Her Majesty sometimes inclined to show temper. This once occurred at Balmoral.

Prior to 1861 the Queen and Prince Consort always dined with the suite when in the Highlands. They sat together at one side of the table, the Prince on the right of the Queen, while the seat on Her Majesty's left—when there was no guest of royal or very exalted rank—was reserved for the minister in attendance. On the occasion to which I refer Lord Palmerston was resolved not to sit next the Queen, and as the party assembled for dinner he slipped into my father's usual place, leaving him without a vacant chair except that next Her Majesty, which of course he was not at liberty

to take except by her command. After a very
uncomfortable minute or two, the lady-in-waiting—
Lady Churchill I think it was—observed his position, and with kind and ready tact moved next the
Queen herself, and motioned my father to take
her place. Lord Palmerston calmly ate his dinner
without apology or explanation.

After the death of the Prince Consort the
Queen always dined in the library with the
members of her family ; guests, and the ladies
and gentlemen of the suite, two or three at a time,
being at Her Majesty's pleasure generally invited
to join her select circle.

I may have seen the Prince Consort during the
last year of his life, but I cannot recall having done
so.

Mr. Anderson, the minister of Crathie, had one
of those curious presentiments regarding the
Prince, to which some natures are susceptible, on
the last occasion on which he saw him in 1861.
Mr. Anderson had gone, as was his custom, to the
gate leading to the Manse to have a last look at
the royal party as they drove away, and the
Prince, apparently in his usual health, had waved

a farewell to him. As he did so Mr. Anderson, who was much attached to the Prince, felt an overwhelming conviction that he was looking upon His Royal Highness for the last time, and he returned home in such deep distress that it was remarked upon by several members of his family, who rallied him for his unaccountable depression. He was unable to shake off the feeling for several days, but his presentiment was that he himself would be the one taken, and not the Prince, who was in the prime of manhood.

Of the sad change which the death of her beloved husband made in the life of the Queen, of the overwhelming grief which threatened for a time to crush even her brave spirit, and of the courage with which she took up her heavy burden of duty and bore it nobly and alone to the end, the whole world knows, and for it a grateful nation will ever bless her memory.

Though during his lifetime there were not wanting carping and slanderous tongues to attack the conduct and spotless character of the Prince Consort, yet the British people, as a whole, heartily joined in the mourning of their Sovereign. It was only after the Prince was taken away that the majority of the nation realised what they had lost, and year by year their appreciation of his great gifts and noble, self-effacing nature has since increased. This was clearly foreseen by Dr. Norman McLeod, who, writing to my father of the short biographical sketch of the Prince by Sir Arthur Helps, says :—

Like everything which Helps writes, it is very clear, simple, elegant, and truthful. But we will have nothing like a worthy portrait of the whole man until we and others who have seen the living original, and gazed on it with love and admiration, have ourselves departed out of sight. The next generation will know and appreciate the Prince better than the present one ever did or can do.

On the 21st August, 1862, the Queen laid the foundation stone of a memorial cairn to the Prince Consort at the top of Craig Laurachen, a rugged hill which rises behind Crathie village. In her *Journal*, she touchingly says :—

I and my poor six orphans all placed stones on it; and our initials, as well as those of the three absent ones, are to be carved on stones all round it. . . . The view was so fine, the day so bright, and the heather so beautifully pink, but no pleasure, no joy, all dead !

The pyramid, thirty-five feet in height, bears the following inscription :—

TO THE BELOVED MEMORY

OF

ALBERT, THE GREAT AND GOOD
PRINCE CONSORT.

RAISED BY HIS BROKEN-HEARTED WIDOW

VICTORIA R.

AUGUST 21, 1862.

" He, being made perfect in a short time, fulfilled a long time :
For His soul pleased the Lord :
Therefore hasted He to take him
Away from among the wicked."—*Wisdom of Solomon*, iv. 13, 14.

A sharp controversy, led by the late Rev. Dr. Candlish, of Free St. George's, Edinburgh, raged for a time round this quotation, highly appropriate most people would think, to the brief, noble life commemorated. The Queen was severely taken to task in some Scottish newspapers for inscribing on this lone hill top, where a quotation from Tennyson or Browning would have passed unnoticed, verses from the Apocrypha instead of the Bible! If we in this new century have lost a little of the religious fervour of forty years ago, we have certainly gained much in breadth of view and larger hope, for no such controversy would now be possible.

It may be interesting to quote in this connection from a letter written to the Queen by her eldest daughter, then Princess Frederick William of Prussia, a few days after the death of the Prince Consort, which Her Majesty graciously permitted my father to copy. It shows that the Princess and not the Queen selected the quotation as specially suitable for the epitaph of the beloved Prince :—

God comes to our aid. My broken, bleeding heart finds support in Him alone. Sorrow such as this I never knew. Earth and all that belongs to it seems so small, so unimportant. My dear beloved Mama, how dear, how kind of you to write to me such a dear, such a beautiful letter—if darling papa had seen it, he would have been proud of you—of your strength of mind. . . . My love, my admiration for him is a part of my existence, cease for a moment it cannot; I was born with it, I inherited it from you, I shall die with it. Oh, dear papa, how great, how good, how faultless! My whole heart and soul was devoted to him. Oh, dear beloved Mama, do not grieve—I hear his voice saying, I am happy—God is a God of love. Let his epitaph be taken from the Wisdom of Solomon, chapter iv. verses 13 and 14, "He being made perfect," etc.

What father could desire a nobler tribute from such a daughter?

Some words of Dr. Taylor, though he came to Crathie as minister of the parish nearly five years after the death of the Prince Consort, have always seemed to me singularly descriptive of the life and aims of His Royal Highness. The occasion on which they were spoken was as follows.

One of the greatest ornaments of the interior of Balmoral Castle is a beautiful marble statue of the Prince, executed by Mr. Theed, the well-known sculptor, some time before the death of His Royal Highness. Of this the Queen had an enlarged copy cast in bronze, which she presented to the tenants and servants on the estate, as a mark of her appreciation of the respect and affection which had induced them—soon after the Prince's death—to erect an obelisk to his memory in the grounds of Balmoral. The bronze statue, which is ten feet in height, was placed near one of the entrances to the castle, in what is now called in the district "the Monument Park," as it contains so many memorials of the good and great who have passed away.

The day fixed for the unveiling of the statue was

the 15th October, 1867, chosen by Her Majesty as being the twenty-eighth anniversary of the day on which she plighted her troth to the husband whom to the last she so tenderly mourned.   My quotation is from the prayer which Dr. Taylor then offered up :—

Especially do we praise Thee at this present for the influence and example of the great and good Prince, the fair proportions of whose life are recalled by the circumstances in which we meet.   In this place, henceforth sacred to his memory, and in the midst of this assembly, holding him in grateful and affectionate remembrance, we do praise Thee for the good work accomplished by him in his time.   Not in full age, as a shock of corn cometh in his season, didst Thou take him, alike from every joy and trouble of this mortal life.   Yet would we praise Thee for that ripeness of wisdom and love of truth, for the devotion to duty and the purity of life which have lengthened the shortness of his time.   Here also would we bless Thee for that benign influence of his, far reaching to every branch of the nation's industry, and to every province of the nation's power, by which he yet speaketh.   O God, who raisest up men by whom nations are exalted, and who willest that the righteous should be held in everlasting remembrance, grant that now, and in the generations to come, the power of his life be for guidance and for encouragement and for strength to kings and governors and

STATUE OF H.R.H. THE PRINCE CONSORT

To face p. 58

humble men.   And, wherein, denying himself, he walked
in the footsteps of Him who humbled Himself, and made
Himself of no reputation, may we also follow him.

Writing to my father a few days later, Mr. Theed
says :—

Anyone who had the good fortune to be personally
known to the great and good Prince, must have a
hard heart who could read the account of the ceremony
without tears.   The prayer was so exquisitely beautiful,
and how true !

After the first dark year of overwhelming grief
brighter news reached us, and it seemed as if in
this rally the grandchildren of the Queen bore a
part, for it often happens, I think, that the stricken
heart is roused to live anew in the young lives
growing up around.

In the spring of 1863 the Grand Duke and
Grand Duchess of Hesse visited Her Majesty at
Windsor Castle, and there the first child of the
Princess Alice was born.   Writing of the event,
Lady Augusta Bruce says :—

The Queen is the most judicious of nurses, certainly the
most kind, attentive, and devoted.   Her Majesty is
certainly much better.   What a blessing it is to see and

acknowledge it! Blessed Queen! there never was such a
character, I think.

She adds :—

The dear young couple are as happy as the day is long,
always occupied, always together; in short, seeming to
inherit the tradition of happy domestic life, thank God!

After the death of the Prince Consort the Queen
commenced those early summer visits to Scotland,
which she found of so much benefit to her health,
and which, in addition to her longer autumn
sojourns, continued uninterruptedly until her death.
They usually lasted a month—from the middle of
May till the middle of June—and as there were
fewer visitors to Deeside so early in the season
these were times of great rest and refreshment to
her.

From this time it seemed as if every action of
her life were even more influenced by the Prince—
by what she believed to be his principles and
wishes—than when he was in bodily form by her
side. This was pre-eminently the case with regard
to Balmoral, which she looked upon very specially
as a memorial of him.

Her Majesty now took the management of the

property more directly into her own hands. Formerly all correspondence with my father was conducted by the gentleman who held the office of Keeper of the Privy Purse, or by Her Majesty's private secretary, but now the Queen commenced a regular autograph correspondence with him regarding affairs at Balmoral, which continued until he resigned his office as Commissioner in 1875. These business letters were by command of the Queen returned to her at my father's death, while his family were permitted to retain those of more personal interest. All that she wrote at this time had more or less reference to the great loss which was never long absent from her mind.

I have before me two touching inscriptions from her own hand upon books given to my father. One, *The Principal Speeches and Addresses of H.R.H. the Prince Consort*, given in 1862, bears the following :—

To Dr. Robertson, of Indego,

In recollection of *our* Great and Good Master,

from

His broken-hearted widow,

VICTORIA R.

OSBORNE, *Dec.* 22, 1862.

The other—the first edition of *Leaves from the Journal of our Life in the Highlands*, printed for private circulation only—was given in 1865, and the inscription runs as follows :—

To Dr. Robertson, M.D.,
In recollection of many happy days spent in our
dear Highland Home now for ever past
from V.R.

BALMORAL, *Oct.* 2, 1865.

From the time of their coming to Deeside it had been a wish dear to the heart of the Queen and the Prince to possess a part at least of the beautiful Ballochbuie Forest, which they both warmly admired.   For a considerable time the Queen rented a portion of it which adjoined the Balmoral property, and when in 1878 the proprietor, Colonel Farquharson, consented to sell that part of the forest so long desired by Her Majesty and the beloved Prince, she thus touchingly refers to him in a letter to my father.

OSBORNE, *April* 13*th*, 1878.

The Queen thanks Dr. Robertson for his kind letter. She is indeed pleased to possess the beautiful Ballochbuie which for thirty years she has enjoyed and admired.   But

OLD SCOTCH FIRS IN BALLOCHBUIE FOREST

To face p. 62

it gives her a pang when she thinks how her dear husband wished (and *then* without the *slightest idea* of the *possibility* of such a thing) that it could have been ours, and that now that *He* is gone from this world—to a far better and happier one—this wish should be realised.

The Queen can say one thing, and that is that in her and her children's hands it will be well cared for and protected.

The sorrow through which the Queen had herself passed intensified her sympathy with all who were sad and suffering. In the autumn of 1864 my stepmother had a severe stroke of paralysis, which for three and a half years rendered her a helpless invalid. The Queen was at Balmoral at the time of the seizure, and at once sent Sir William Jenner to give us the aid of his valuable advice, and throughout those anxious years Her Majesty gave practical proof by word and deed of her kind thought for those in trouble. In January, 1865, our invalid became for a time alarmingly worse, and the Queen wrote to my father :—

OSBORNE, *January 28th*, 1865.

The Queen has learned with the deepest concern of Mrs. Robertson's alarming and distressing state, and wishes herself to express to Dr. Robertson her most heartfelt sympathy. One who, like herself, has drunk so deeply of the cup of sorrow knows how to *feel*, and does feel acutely for the sufferings and misfortunes of others ; and Dr. Robertson may be assured that *no* one grieves more truly for him than she does. She would still venture to hope that there might be a change for the better, and that the valuable life of Mrs. Robertson might yet be spared to him. May God support him and his daughter under this severe trial.

I shall never forget the gentle, womanly kindness of the Queen on one occasion, when, accompanied by the Princess Christian and Lady Churchill, she paid a special visit of sympathy to my poor mother, who, though recognising her august guest, was unable to speak, or even to rise from her chair to receive her. An amusing incident, I remember, relieved the sadness of the visit, and afforded Her Majesty a hearty laugh.

A little nephew about three years old was with us, and had on a pair of red shoes, of which he was not a little proud. He at once called attention to them, asking, "Do you like my pretty new shoes ? I got them because the Queen was coming."

When death released my mother from her

suffering state, Her Majesty addressed another letter of kind sympathy to my father.

BALMORAL, *May 30th*, 1868.

The Queen has just learnt with deep concern of the sad termination of his beloved wife's long and distressing illness, and the Queen is anxious to express her very sincerest sympathy with Dr. Robertson.

The Queen knows how devoted Dr. Robertson was to his dear wife, and she to him, and though he was to a great extent deprived by her suffering state of her assistance and companionship, he had the satisfaction of nursing her and of knowing what a happiness his presence was to her. All who had the pleasure of knowing Mrs. Robertson had the greatest regard for her, and she will be much regretted.

That God may support Dr. Robertson in his hour of heavy affliction is the Queen's earnest prayer.

The following week she wrote again, the Friday alluded to being the day of my mother's funeral.

BALMORAL.

The Queen hopes Dr. Robertson is feeling tolerably well. She thought much of him on Friday.

Princess Christian begged the Queen to express her warmest sympathy with Dr. Robertson in his sad loss.

F

During the remaining years of my father's tenure of office as Commissioner few events of importance occurred at Balmoral.

Improvements were always in progress; new cottages, new roads, new bridges—everything, indeed, that the best of landlords could do for the comfort and well-being of the people.

Marriages and births occurred in the Royal Family, and were celebrated right merrily in the usual fashion at Balmoral by dinners, balls, and bonfires, but there was little specially to record. Her Majesty's health and spirits improved, and she was always happy in her Highland home. She had a keen sense of humour, and thoroughly enjoyed a good story. One of her ladies told me she always treasured up any she heard, to amuse the Queen when she was in-waiting and they were out driving together. The late Dowager Duchess of Athole, to whom the Queen was much attached, was an excellent *raconteuse*. I have often heard my father speak of the Queen's intense amusement on one occasion when he was present and the Duchess told the story of the comical advertisement regarding the Dunkeld and Blair-

gowrie coach, which was once posted in the village
of Dunkeld. The coach was named "The Duchess
of Athole" and the inn from which it started was
the "Duke's Arms." The notice ran as follows:
"'The Duchess of Athole' leaves 'The Duke's
Arms' every lawful morning at six o'clock!"

Of those ladies and gentlemen who formed the
suite generally in attendance upon the Queen at
Balmoral during the years of which I write nearly
all have passed away. Some of the younger ladies
remain to mourn their beloved Royal Mistress,
but I think the Dowager Countess of Erroll is the
only lady-in-waiting now alive who was much
at Balmoral then, and even she did not belong
to the first ten or fifteen years of the Queen's
residence there.

The only gentlemen I can recall as still living are
Lord Bridport and my father's kind and true friend,
the Duke of Grafton, then Lord Charles Fitzroy.

Her Majesty had the gift of wise selection, and
only surrounded herself with those who were worthy
of the honour. Of all with whom my father had
business or social relations he had only good to
say, and to many he was warmly attached.

During the last ten years of his life he was a good deal with the late Duke of Albany when at Balmoral. H.R.H.'s health at that time often precluded his taking part in the more active life of the Court. He frequently dined and spent the evening in his own rooms, and collected round him a little circle of his own, for talk, or a quiet rubber of whist. Mr.— afterwards Sir Robert—Collins and Mr. Sahl were always with the Prince, and sometimes Canon Duckworth, Sir William Jenner, or my father. Generally once during the season His Royal Highness and some of the gentlemen I have mentioned drove down to Indego or Hopewell to lunch with us, and very merry times these were.

Practical joking of a kindly sort often went on, for the Prince, when in fair health, was full of fun, as well as a most interesting, well-informed companion in discussing more serious subjects, giving his opinion very thoughtfully and quietly. "The Untravelled Traveller," as Dean Stanley styles him, had gathered richly from the realms of art and literature in his hours of enforced leisure, and an inward strength and power from that threefold experience of the Valley of the Shadow of Death, from which he returned for too brief a time to earthly light and life.

In 1875 my father, feeling the weight of advanced years, asked Her Majesty's permission to retire from her service. The following extracts from her letters on this subject will show Her Majesty's appreciation of faithful service, and her regard for my father personally :—

BALMORAL, *October 4th*, 1875.

The Queen is very anxious to know how Dr. Robertson is, and trusts that the quiet of Hopewell will have made him feel stronger and better. She, however, feels from what he said to her yesterday, and from what he said last year, that he has a right to be relieved from the duties he has so long and ably performed, and which must be too fatiguing for him now. She wishes his successor to reside on the estate, so as to be always on the spot, and not to belong to *the Household.* . . . The Queen would wish to express her very warm thanks to Dr. Robertson for his devotion to the dear Prince's and her service during twenty-seven years, and her hope that she may yet have the pleasure of seeing him from time to time. Everything has in fact been done here, and it only requires to be carefully carried on and the Queen's wishes attended to.

BALMORAL, *October 5th*, 1875.

The Queen acknowledges Dr. Robertson's letter received this evening, and is glad to hear he is better, and likely to be able soon to come over. It will be to the Queen also a source of sincere regret to see Dr. Robertson retire, after having been for so many years in her dear husband's and her service, but she would be more grieved did she not think that his life will be prolonged by the relief from responsibility and anxiety, as well as from exposure to fatigue and cold in the winter. . . . The Queen hopes to go over to Hopewell in the end of this week.

Dr. Profeit was appointed as successor to my father, and a pretty residence was built near Balmoral for his accommodation.

My father retained his appointment as Commissioner to H.R.H. the Prince of Wales, our present gracious King, until within a short time of his death in 1881.

During his last illness the kind solicitude of Her Majesty and other members of the Royal Family was most gratifying and touching, and I shall never forget the sad visit of inquiry and sympathy paid by the Sovereign to her dying servant within a few weeks of his death.

He was able to be at the entrance to receive her, and she strove to cheer him with kindly words of hope, but both knew that in all human probability they met for the last time. I feel that I cannot more fittingly close this chapter upon Balmoral and my father's connection with it than by giving copies of three telegrams which I received on the sad day of his death—tributes to him which, coming from our late revered Sovereign and our present beloved King and Queen, could not fail to be deeply gratifying to his children.

TELEGRAMS.

From the Queen, Balmoral,
To Mrs. Lindsay, 16, Bonnacord Square, Aberdeen.

Deeply grieved to hear the news your brother has just telegraphed, and wish you, your brother, and sister to accept the expression of my sincere sympathy and regret.

From H.R.H. the Prince of Wales, Rendlesham, to the same.

I sympathise sincerely with you on the loss of your dear father. Most sincerely shall I ever regret so kind and valued a friend.

From H.R.H. the Princess of Wales, Sandringham, to the same.

I am most deeply grieved at the sad tidings of your dear father's death which reached us to-night. Feel most truly for you all.

To these I add a copy of one of my most treasured possessions, the autograph letter written to me the following day by Her late Majesty :—

BALMORAL CASTLE, *November 17, 1881.*

DEAR MRS. LINDSAY,—Tho' I telegraphed to you yesterday, I wish to write to express to you and your brother and sister my true sympathy with you in the irreparable loss of your beloved father, whose last days you have all helped to cheer. I wish also to express my deep regret at the loss of one who was so bound up with former happy days at Balmoral and with all connected with this, my beloved Highland home!

He will ever be remembered by me in connection with my dear husband and the creation of this beautiful place as it now exists.

Believe me,
Yours sincerely,
VICTORIA, R. and I.

Princess Beatrice wishes to join in my expressions of sympathy and regret.

Would you let me have the latest photograph of dear Dr. Robertson?

CHAPTER IV

ABERGELDIE CASTLE

" When I remember all
    The friends so linked together,
I've seen around me fall
    Like leaves in wintry weather ;
I feel like one who treads alone
    Some banquet-hall deserted,
Whose lights are fled, whose garlands dead,
    And all but he departed !
Thus in the stilly night,
    Ere slumber's chain has bound me,
Fond memory brings the light
    Of other days around me."—MOORE.

The Gordon family—Lease of Abergeldie by the Queen—The old garden—
    The cradle—Tragic incident—Story of the larch—The Abergeldie ghost
    —Murdoch's cairn—Story of "the black hand"—The Duchess of Kent
    —Recollections of Her Royal Highness—Ladies and gentlemen of her
    suite—Character of the Duchess—Her death in 1861—Subsequent tenants
    —Birkhall—Altnaguischach—Glassalt Shiel.

AMONG the surroundings of Balmoral none have
occupied such an important place in the life of the
Royal Family as Abergeldie Castle. Situated on
the south bank of the Dee, about two miles from
Balmoral, it consists of an old keep with walls of

73

great thickness, and various more or less harmoni-
ous modern additions. It has been owned for
some centuries by a branch of the Huntly family,
but within my recollection the castle has never
been occupied by a Gordon. The succession to
the property for the last sixty years has followed a
curiously erratic course. David Gordon, the 14th
laird, settled the estate during his lifetime upon
his eldest son Charles, and retired to Birkhall.
Whether such a deed, dealing with an entailed
property, was valid may be open to question, but
it was virtually acted upon. Charles predeceased
his father, leaving no son, and was succeeded by
his brother Michael, their father David being still
alive. This Michael Gordon, whose wife was a
sister of my stepmother, was the first laird of
Abergeldie whom I remember; he survived his
four sons and was followed by his brother, Admiral
Gordon, a bachelor. At his death a nephew
became proprietor; he too has now passed away
childless, and the estate has descended to his
brother. As he has more than one son, we may
hope the order which has prevailed for so long may
now give place to a more direct succession.

The Queen and Prince Consort greatly desired to add Abergeldie to their Highland property, and many were the advantageous offers of purchase made to the Gordon family and persistently declined. These efforts having failed, the castle and estate were rented by the Queen on a forty years' lease, subsequently renewed for a period of nineteen years. It thus became practically her own for life, and considerable sums were laid out upon the place—the house enlarged, roads made, cottages and schools built—and in every way the same generous help and kindness extended to the Abergeldie tenants as to those on the Balmoral property. The castle has a charming old garden, with a spreading copper beech and delicious old "gean" trees,* broad grass walks, and sweet, old-fashioned flowers. What a happy playground it was to us children, and how kind and forbearing were old Andrew Wilson and his assistant, Johnnie Mc Dougal! Andrew has long lain beneath the earth he tended so lovingly, and Johnnie has for many years been presiding genius of the old garden. He too is getting on in life, and is one of the very

* A tall tree of the cherry species, well known in Scotland.

few remaining of the old servants I remember in
the early days of the Queen's sojourn on Deeside.
To those who loved the soothing ripple or swish of
the many-voiced river there was a still more delightful haunt beyond the north wall of the garden,
the green terrace along the river-side, where used
to stand the cradle, in my time the only means of
communication with the north bank between the
bridges of Ballater and Crathie. By the cradle
letters and parcels were brought to Abergeldie, and
many visitors crossed merely to enjoy the exciting
novelty of the transit. A strong cable spanned the
river, wound round a sort of windlass at either end.
On this ran the cradle, which consisted of three
narrow planks connected by iron bands, curved like
the rockers of a cradle. At the ends were wooden
uprights, with a crossbar at the top, and beneath
this two grooved iron wheels which ran along the
cable. The cradle was large enough to seat two
people, and the castle gardener, who usually worked
it, placed one leg across the knees of the passengers
to keep them steady. A merry run was made to
the middle of the river, and then by grasping the
cable, the cradle with its burden was hauled up on

ABERGELDIE CASTLE (back view)

To face p. 76

the other side.   To my childish imagination the cradle was always associated with the tragic fate of a young couple who were drowned when crossing in it—I think on the evening of their wedding day. They had been entertained in the castle kitchen, and were returning home, the bridegroom taking his bride in the cradle, when suddenly the spoke of the windlass gave way, causing the rope to uncoil and swing back with great violence, pitching the unfortunate pair into the river, which was in high flood at the time.   The accident occurred in the early part of last century, and I have often heard the story from those who remembered pretty Ba'bie Brown, "The Flower of Deeside," as she was called, and Willie Frankie, her stalwart gamekeeper husband.   The cradle itself is now among the many "things that are no more," and its place is supplied by a chain footbridge.

On the lawn in front of the castle stands one of the oldest larches on Deeside, and a curious history attached to it in my young days.   The first trees of this kind were brought to Scotland from Norway, more than a hundred years ago, by the Duke of Athole, who planted them at Dunkeld, where some fine specimens are still standing. The Duke gave some seedlings in pots to the laird of Invercauld, who was proud of the rare plants, and showed them to the laird of Abergeldie on the occasion of his next visit. Years passed, and one day, when calling at Abergeldie, Mr. Gordon showed him a finer larch than any of his own. "Where got ye that, Abergeldie?" said the irate Farquharson. "'Deed it's just ane o' yours, Invercauld, that I put i' my pouch lang syne," replied Gordon, with the unabashed spirit of the Highland cateran of an earlier day. It has been said that stolen goods rarely prosper, but there stands the larch a living contradiction, or possibly the exception that proves the rule. Near the tree is a curious upright stone, which was an object of interest, not to say alarm, in my youth, from its likeness in the dusk to a veiled grey figure, or a modern Lot's wife. The servants about the place used to call it "Lady Portman," whom they declared it resembled. Lord Portman and his family occupied Abergeldie Castle one of the early years of the Queen's stay at Balmoral—1849 I think.

Abergeldie was not without its ghost—hardly to

be called a family one, but local certainly. It
was that of Kitty Rankine, of whose history
nothing is known, except the tradition that she was
confined for some time in one of the cellars of the
castle, from which she was taken to be burnt on
Craig-na-Ban as a witch. Kitty's dungeon, with
its little door just high enough for a child of ten to
stand upright on the threshold, had a delightful
fascination for me, and, though frequently visited
with pleasure by day, was much to be avoided after
dark. Old Effie, the first housekeeper I remember
at the castle, used to tell us blood-curdling tales of
mysterious noises and bell-ringings, supposed to
augur misfortune to the Gordon family; but to my
regret she could never be induced to say that she
had actually seen the spook of Kitty the Witch.

Superstition was still pretty strong on Deeside in
the middle of last century, and there was one spot
in the Craig-Guise woods which few cared to pass
after nightfall. A man of the name of Murdoch,
a sort of gipsy or tramp, had been murdered there
long ago, and his ghost was supposed to haunt the
cairn which commemorated the dark deed. It was
currently reported that he was seen at times by

belated travellers, but these occasions corresponded curiously with the Ballater markets. Long-legged, loose-jointed Jamie Robertson of the Tammieduise used graphically to describe his encounter with the ghost: "As I cam hame frae Ballater, I saw Murdoch sittin' upo' the cairn, girnin' at me, jist himsel' and nae ither, clouted claes and a'. I winna say I wisna' *some* feared, but I widna rin. Na! I wid *no* rin, I widna pleesure him by rinnin', but it *wid* hae been a swack man that wid hae owerta'en me i' the Craig-Guise that nicht."

A curious incident, illustrative of the old Highland superstition that stolen iron never rests where hidden, has been told me on good authority as occurring in Crathie in the old smuggling days. Two men went to the mill of Inver to dry some malt in the kiln, an errand of not unfrequent occurrence, and it was always done at night for fear of the exciseman. They took it in turn to watch the fire and keep it at a proper heat, and while one watched, the other lay down to rest on a heap of empty sacks behind the door. In this door was a hole, left for the passing in and out of the cat, kept no doubt like the immortal Jack's, "to kill the rat that ate the malt." While the man on the sacks slept, the watcher saw a black hand come through the hole and drop a stone on the chest of the sleeper. He stirred and asked what was wanted. "Nothing," said the other, "go to sleep." This occurred a second time, with only the result of increased irritability on the part of the sleeper, who thought he was being made the subject of a practical joke. When however the hand appeared for the third time, the watcher told the other what had happened, and advised him to go out, as he was evidently wanted. He declined, so the man at the fire said, "If you won't I will, and if I don't come back, you can tell my folk how I went."

On going out he saw the black figure of a man, who retreated as he advanced, and led the way to a ruined house and old garden not far distant. Here he stopped, and pointing to the ground, said, "Dig there," and disappeared. The man who followed marked the spot, and dug accordingly the next morning. About three feet below the surface he found an old sword-hilt with the blade broken in half.

The black hand was not seen again. The man

G

who told this story, whom I remember well, was grandson to him who followed the figure, and used to say he had often seen the old sword, and played with it as a boy, but did not know what had become of it.

From 1850 to 1858 Abergeldie Castle was the autumn residence of Her late Royal Highness the Duchess of Kent, who loved the place, and was in turn beloved by all there who came within the influence of her kindly and gracious presence. I first saw Her Royal Highness in 1850, when she honoured my parents with a visit on her way to, or from, Haddo House.

I think the Duchess must have been handsome in her youth, for I can still call up from that long-past day the image of a stout, comely, elderly lady, whose face overflowed with kindliness and good humour, quietly dignified, yet with a gentle courtesy that set even a shy child at ease. The Duchess usually came to Deeside earlier than the Queen, and during those few weeks there was less of ceremony and Court etiquette about the life at Abergeldie. After 1854 "The Mains" was a second home to us, and when there the Duchess frequently

Walker & Cockerell, ph. sc.

The Duchess of Kent and Prince Alfred.

invited my sister and me, though still in the schoolroom, to accompany our elders to dine and spend the evening at the castle. Those occasions are happy memories to me now, but at the time I hardly know whether pleasure or nervousness predominated, for to shy, half-grown girls, who rarely left home, dining at a royal table was somewhat of an ordeal. Before the evening was half over, however, I am sure pleasure was well to the front, owing to the sympathy and kindness always shown to us. The Duchess had the true German love of music, and frequently played on the piano in the drawing - room after dinner. " Patience " was also a favourite amusement of hers, and occasionally there was a rubber of whist. To us young ones the crowning delight was a ball night. There were some royal birthdays in August, Her Royal Highness's own among the number, and on these anniversaries there was generally a dance given to the tenants and servants. The Duchess and her party sat on a raised platform at the end of the long dining-room, which was cleared for dancing as soon as we left the dinner-table. It was a good room for the purpose, and

from the walls the rather grim Gordons of earlier
generations looked down upon the revelry.   On
these occasions the Duchess always wore white, and,
though at this time she must have been approach-
ing seventy, it was still becoming to her.   On her
head was always a cap of lace and ribbons, a
genuine cap of the old-fashioned type, which the
youthful old ladies of the present day have dis-
carded.   At these dances we girls and the younger
ladies in attendance on the Duchess always wore
silk or satin tartan scarves, fixed on the shoulder,
Highland fashion, over our white or black dresses.
We had the privilege of selecting our partners
from among scarlet-coated, powdered footmen and
kilted keepers and ghillies; and reels, country dances,
and the "everlasting jig" succeeded each other in
quick succession to the inspiring strains of the bag-
pipes or Willie Blair's fiddle.   The Duchess sat
smiling kindly upon the pleasure of her guests of
all degrees, and evidently enjoying the merriment,
which her presence always kept within due bounds.
Before midnight the Duchess bade a kindly good
night to the company; and we hurried home through
the old garden, full of ghostly shadows in the moon-

light, or, if the moon failed us, sometimes taking an erratic course through strawberry beds and gooseberry bushes in a darkness that might be felt.

When I call to mind the charming circle which was gathered round the Duchess in those old days, a goodly company rises before me—all, I think, now passed away. A sprightly old German Baroness de Spaet, full of lively sallies in her quaint broken English, often pretending to misunderstand in order to raise a laugh at her own expense. I recall also an elderly lady-in-waiting devoted to dogs, and firmly believing in their possession of souls and prospect of a future life—an opinion much strengthened, she told me, by having once seen the ghost of Lambkin, the Duchess's white poodle, after that royal favourite had departed for the happy hunting-grounds of his race.

Grave, kind Sir George Couper, H.R.H.'s Master of the Household, belonged to the earlier years at Abergeldie; latterly his place there was taken by Lord James Murray, brother of the late, and uncle of the present, Duke of Athole; a tall, handsome man, who had served with the Guards

in the Crimea ; a good soldier, an admirable Highland dancer, and, above all, an ever - courteous
gentleman.

Of Lady James, too, I have grateful recollections ; and of big, kind Mr. Tom Bruce, whose
reel dancing was elephantine, and, like himself,
demanded much space. But of all the pleasant
circle none has such a place in my heart and
memory as his sister, Lady Augusta Bruce, afterwards the much-loved, deeply mourned wife of
Dean Stanley. From my childhood she was my
ideal of all a woman ought to be, bright and
clever in conversation and repartee, yet ever con-
siderate of the feelings of others, and trying to
bring out all the best that was in them ; earnestly
good and spiritual, yet enjoying life, and striving
always to make others happy. She was not
pretty, but her tall, graceful figure, keen, dark eyes,
and bright, intelligent expression more than re-
deemed an otherwise plain face. Lady Augusta
was true to the core, and ever had a hearty welcome for her friends either on this side the Channel,
or in Paris, where, until the death of her mother,
the Dowager Lady Elgin, she spent those months

of the year that she was not "in waiting." How
many sojourners in Paris, like myself, and still
more my brother, have grateful, happy recollections
of the old house in the Quartier St. Germain,
where Lady Augusta gathered round her all that
was best and most cultured of French society, as
she afterwards did of English in the Deanery at
Westminster.

Early in the summer of 1859 the shadow began
to fall, and many feared, only too truly, that the
dear Duchess would no more go in and out
amongst us as in past years. In June Sir George
Couper wrote to my father :—

Her Majesty wishes everything to be kept prepared
for H.R.H. going to Abergeldie in August. Would I
could think she would do so ! . . . Her Majesty's anxiety
and tender affection for Her Royal Highness is most
touching.

Though unable to pay her usual visit to Abergeldie, the Duchess's care for the poor on the
estate did not fail, for on August 9th, 1859, Sir
George Couper wrote :—

I have received your letter of the 4th inst. from Her
Royal Highness with the following message : "I return

dear Dr. Robertson's letter, and he may be assured that I feel the greatest regret not to be with them this year· It is a great sacrifice to me not to go. Be so good as to tell him that I am very anxious that all the poor celebrate my birthday as usual, and receive what they have been in the habit of receiving.

In the autumns of 1859 and 1860 the Duchess rented a place near Edinburgh, the journey to Abergeldie being considered too much for her failing strength. In March, 1861, as we all know, the end came somewhat suddenly at Frogmore, and there passed away a wise, noble, and devout spirit, firm and true to her convictions of right, one to whom the nation owes much, and in every way worthy to be the mother of the great and good Queen who has but recently followed her to the Silent Land. It was the first great sorrow of the Queen's life, and was deeply felt, but she often said that she thanked God for that bitter experience, as it helped her to bear the overwhelming bereavement which befell her ere the year closed.

The following letter from Lady Augusta Bruce, then in constant attendance upon the Queen, shows Her Majesty's sympathetic spirit, as well as Lady

ABERGELDIE CASTLE (front view)

To face p. 88

Augusta's devotion to the Duchess and the Highland home where they had spent so many happy days together. The book alluded to was a translation of some German hymns sent to my father by the Queen.

July 14th, 1861.

DEAR DR. ROBERTSON,—The Queen sends you the accompanying volume, which will tell its own tale. The original German collection was constantly used by our beloved Duchess, and these selected poems were some which seemed to the Queen full of a comfort which Her Majesty was anxious others should share with herself. . . . I rejoice to think that I am to see you in Aberdeenshire. It will bring back much of the past to be there again, but all these memories are precious, and so comforting to dwell on. . . .   Yours most truly,

AUGUSTA BRUCE.

After the marriage of H.R.H. the Prince of Wales, Abergeldie became his Highland residence, and when unoccupied by him, its tenants were many and varied, including the ex-Empress of the French, the Duc d'Aumale, and others of more or less note ; but my happiest recollections of Abergeldie Castle cluster round the days when the Duchess of Kent held her Court within its walls.

The property of Abergeldie extends some three

or four miles down the river below the castle, on
the south bank, and the road winds at the foot of
the beautifully wooded hills of Craig-na-Ban and
Craig-Guise until it reaches the Bridge of Girnoc,
where a neat school was built by the Prince Consort
some fifty years ago.   Nearly a mile below this
the Abergeldie property marches with Birkhall,
which also belonged to the Gordon family.   Soon
after the Queen first came to Deeside it was bought
for the Prince of Wales, but some years ago it was
repurchased from him by Her Majesty.

The house is beautifully situated, but it is too
small for a royal residence, and to the best of my
recollection was only once occupied by the Prince,
the year before his marriage, 1862.

For many seasons Sir James Clark, the Queen's
physician, and his family resided there ; and latterly
it was generally tenanted by the family of some
gentleman connected with the Court.

A beautiful drive up the River Muick leads to
Alt-na-guischach, or "The Hut," as it used to be
called, a cottage considerably enlarged by the
Queen, where she and the Prince Consort, with
usually one lady and gentleman in attendance, used

to resort for a day or two at a time, for greater
privacy and quiet enjoyment of the beautiful
scenery of Loch Muick. Many a happy day I
have spent at Loch Muick, and have vivid recollections of its trout and its midges, both superlative
in their way. I think it was an evening at Alt-na-
guischach that inspired one of the party with his
epigrammatic description of the origin of the
Highland fling—" A kilt and midges !"

Some years later the Queen built a beautiful
shooting-lodge at the Glassalt, on the upper shore
of Loch Muick, under the shadow of Loch-na-gar,
one of the many additions made by her to the
Abergeldie property.

CHAPTER V

"CONCERNING THINGS ECCLESIASTICAL"

" Through aisles of long-drawn centuries
   My spirit walks in thought,
And to that symbol lifts its eyes
   Which God's own pity wrought ;
From Calvary shines the altar's gleam,
   The Church's East is there,
The Ages one great Minster seem
   That throbs with praise and prayer.

" Moravian hymn and Roman chant
   In one devotion blend,
To speak the soul's eternal want
   Of Him, the inmost friend ;
One prayer soars cleansed with martyr fire,
   One choked with sinner's tears,
In heaven both meet in one desire,
   And God one music hears."—LOWELL.

Pre-Reformation church—Early ecclesiastical history of Crathie—The four
   chapels—The two Fergussons—The author of *Sherriff-Muir*—Second
   parish church—"The beadle"—Celebrated preachers—A pulpit story—
   Memorial windows—Dr. Norman McLeod—Letter of the Queen on his
   death—Principal Caird—Annual Sacrament Sunday—The Queen's first
   Communion in the Scottish Church—Mr. Anderson—Towser—Later
   clergymen—First Free Church—Lord Dalhousie—Dr. Guthrie—Later
   churches.

THREE parish churches of Crathie have existed in
whole or in part within my recollection.

The oldest — of which the ivy-covered ruin remains a picturesque feature in the churchyard— is known to have been of pre-Reformation date, but the exact time at which it was built is uncertain. It was dedicated to St. Manirus, or Manaire, probably a local saint, as a pool on the Dee, known as Polmanaire, still commemorates his name. He may be looked upon therefore as the first traditional incumbent of Crathie.

Prior to the Reformation the church of Crathie belonged to the Abbey of Cambus-Kenneth, near Stirling—a long distance, one would think, in those days for any direction of its spiritual concerns to be kept up, but it was usual, and indeed necessary in troublous times, for poor outlying Highland churches to be under the protection of some rich and powerful ecclesiastical foundation.

The remains of three chapels which had existed before the Reformation are to be found in different parts of the parish, and tradition has it that a fourth stood on " Balmurrell" (Balmoral), but nothing certain is known of it.

Of those still to be traced, one was at Micras, a small hamlet on the north bank of the Dee, nearly opposite Abergeldie Castle. Another at Balmore, in Aberarder—also on the north side of the river—has a few stones still *in situ*. The third, on the farm of Mains of Abergeldie, was well known to me, though no remains of the building are now to be seen. It stood within a wooded inclosure in a field always called the chapel park, and is said to have been dedicated to St. Valentine. I remember hearing long ago of un-baptised children being buried there, probably from some lingering belief in the virtue, for such, of consecrated ground. In an old letter to my father from Hill Burton, the historian, written in 1829, there is mention of a chapel at Abergeldie. He wrote to ask my father's aid in tracing Roman remains on upper Deeside, and quotes from an old work, Chalmers's *Caledonia*, where it is said that a certain Captain Macdonald of Gardensdale had showed the author an ancient road, believed to be Roman, which first appeared near the "chapel of Abergeldie," and proceeded northward along the hill of Gailac to Rineton, in Glengairn.

The parishes of Crathie and Braemar had been united from the time of the Reformation, if not earlier, and were only separated in 1879, when Braemar, having largely increased in population and importance, was made a distinct parish. From the Reformation until 1633 there is no record of any settled minister resident in Crathie, and possibly until then the bulk of the scattered population adhered to the old faith. From my earliest recollection there have been considerable numbers of Roman Catholics—if not in Crathie itself—in Braemar on the one side and Glengairn on the other.

In 1633 Alexander Fergusson, whose daughter Agnes married an ancestor of my own, James Farquharson, of Inverey, was minister of Crathie. Many believe, though some links in the chain of evidence are wanting, that from this Mr. Fergusson was descended Robert Fergusson, the Scottish poet, author of *The Farmer's Ingle*, to whom Burns paid a striking tribute on the stone which he erected to the memory of Fergusson in the Canongate churchyard, Edinburgh.

Another Ferguson was minister of Crathie at the time of the rebellion of 1715, a man of influence and a keen politician, best known however as the father of Adam Ferguson, the historian. This Mr. Ferguson was a strong supporter of King George, and after the rebellion was crushed, proved himself a valuable friend at Court to his old parishioner, the laird of Invercauld, who had espoused the Jacobite cause. In acknowledgment of the pardon he had received through the good offices of Mr. Ferguson—then minister of Logie-rait, Perthshire—and at his suggestion, Mr. Farquharson of Invercauld founded a bursary to assist in the education and maintenance of boys of the names of Farquharson, Ferguson, and McDonald. In my young days this bequest was still administered by the Invercauld family for the benefit of the parish of Crathie.

A third minister of Crathie in the latter half of the eighteenth century, the Rev. Murdoch McLennan, was not unknown to literary fame, for to him we owe the ballad of *Sherriff-Muir*. He was a man of considerable attainments and rich in Highland lore, which unfortunately he never committed to paper.

The second parish church of Crathie, hallowed to me by many sacred memories, was built in 1804, during the ministry of the Rev. Charles McHardy. His successor was a Mr. McFarlane, who died in

THE OLD CHURCH OF CRATHIE

To face p. 96

1840, and was followed by my kind old friend Mr. Anderson, who for twenty-six years was minister of the parish.

This church was a foursquare, whitewashed building, "harled," as it is called in Scotland, with a belfry in the centre of the front.

It was one of the sights of Crathie to me in my young days to see little Jamie Gow, very short and rotund, clad in blue homespun, with a broad bonnet on his head, pulling the rope beneath that belfry. The rope was short and the effort apparently great, and I fear I often watched in hope that the force of the pull would hoist Jamie in mid-air when the bell swung back. It always rang from the time the minister started to walk from the Manse up the riverside until he reached the church. There was no vestry, so on fine days he wore his gown, and many were Jamie's anxious looks for the approach of the black-robed figure.

I wonder why country "beddles" in old times were generally oddities, often in appearance as well as character, and sometimes much impressed with the dignity of their office. "*Me* and the minister thinks so-and-so" was not an uncommon preface to

H

an expression of ecclesiastical opinion.   I often think that a history of various notable Scottish beadles of the past—for they are all "Church officers" now, and mostly cut according to pattern— if collected and sketched by one of our clever "word painters" would be very amusing reading.

Perhaps it is their occupation, bringing them into close business relations with the gloomy side of death, what Jamie Gow used to call "howkin the holes," that gives a unique and rather familiarly gruesome tone to the conversation of these "Old Mortalities."   I think Jamie's short stature made him fear that he would get buried himself if he dug the graves of a proper depth, but the sanitary inspector was not abroad in those days, and the occupants slept as soundly within three, as within six feet of the surface of the ground.

The interior of the church was encircled on three sides by a gallery, the front divided into five large deep pews set apart for the five lairds or heritors of the parish.   On the west side were Invercauld and Balmoral, on the east side Mar Lodge and Monaltrie, while Abergeldie occupied the central position opposite the pulpit.

Few buildings have resounded to more eloquence than that little Highland church. Dr. Norman McLeod, Principal Caird, Principal Tulloch, Dr. McGregor, and many others now mostly passed away, have filled its pulpit, and no preachers ever had more attentive or appreciative listeners than the occupants of the royal pew, who when at Balmoral were regular attendants at the parish church. The late Queen has herself testified to the pleasure and comfort derived from what she heard there, and the Prince Consort liked the Scottish service, which he used to say reminded him of the simple Lutheran forms to which in his early youth he was accustomed in Germany. He greatly admired Dr. Caird's preaching, and told my father that with the exception of the late Dr. Samuel Wilberforce, then Bishop of Oxford, he was the most eloquent man he had ever heard in the pulpit.

It was a not unnatural object of ambition to many ministers in the north to preach before the Queen; and to most of the leading men in the Church, and to those who had been Moderators of the General Assembly, this privilege was accorded.

On one such occasion an elderly minister hitherto

unknown to the Queen was to officiate, and she asked my father if he was acquainted with him. He replied in the affirmative, adding that he was an excellent man, highly esteemed in the Church, but that he had a peculiar pronunciation, as, for instance, in the words "Clap your hands" he always said "Clip your hens." By a strange chance the opening psalm selected on the Sunday was the forty-seventh, and my father often told how when the minister stood up and gave out "All people clip your hens," Her Majesty turned round with a humorous glance of appreciative recollection of his story. After the death of Dr. Norman McLeod two windows were placed to his memory in Crathie Church, one by the Queen, the other by Mr. Strahan, the publisher. One represented King David playing on a harp; and an old parishioner, to whom stained-glass windows were a novelty, believed the figure to be a likeness of Dr. McLeod endowed with a heavenly crown and harp, and told me it was a "bonnie pictur but nane like the doctor."

When the church was taken down these windows were carefully preserved, but as their shape did not

suit the architecture of the new building, they have
not yet been refixed.   It is to be hoped that some
way may be found of adapting them, for it seems
a pity that they should not find a place in Crathie
Church, where Dr. McLeod was so well known,
honoured, and loved.

The Queen has herself borne witness to her high
appreciation of his prayers and sermons, and in the
first sad years of her widowhood she gained both
strength and comfort from the conversation of that
large-hearted Christian man.   Surely no subject
ever had a higher tribute from his Sovereign than is
contained in the pages devoted to Dr. McLeod at
the time of his death in Her Majesty's *Journal:*—
"How I loved to talk with him, to ask his advice,
and to speak to him of my sorrows and anxieties.
. . . No one ever raised and strengthened one's faith
more than Dr. McLeod ; his own faith was so strong,
his heart so large, that high and low, weak and
strong, the erring and the good could alike find
sympathy, help, and consolation from him."   What
would not most of us give to be to any friend such
"a cup of strength in some great agony," and how
much more to one whose exalted and isolated

position rendered such ministrations of helpful sympathy far more difficult.

My father represented the Queen at Dr. Mc Leod's funeral, and shortly after she wrote as follows :—

WINDSOR CASTLE, *July 1st,* 1872.

The Queen thanks Dr. Robertson for his interesting and touching letter giving an account of the funeral of our beloved and ever to be lamented Dr. McLeod. It must have been most impressive and affecting. The Queen trusts some day to visit Campsie, and wishes to know how it could be reached. . . . She saw a very full account [of the funeral] in the *Scotsman.* There never was more general regret or appreciation for one in his position before, or hardly indeed in any position.

A generation has now passed, or nearly so, since that stalwart form was laid to rest in Campsie churchyard, and the number is becoming few of those who remember him in the full vigour of his manhood and stirring eloquence. Like Charles Kingsley, he was essentially the Christian *man* first, and the *clergyman* next. None who knew him will ever forget the large, genial face, which crowned what he used jokingly to call "the biggest embodiment of divinity in Scotland," a face lit up—now with the fervour of an apostle—again brimming over with fun, as he told a humorous story in his inimitable fashion—or yet again in the house of mourning when, his eyes dimmed by sympathetic tears, he exercised his almost magnetic power of influence and consolation.

Principal Caird was also an impressive personality, but very different. Of medium height, thin, dark, and close-shaven, he possessed a fine voice and a strikingly thoughtful, intellectual face. He was pre-eminently a student, shy and retiring, but with a true kindness of heart which his reserved nature seldom permitted to come to the surface, but which many found out by practical experience.

Crathie Church is situated on a grassy platform under the shadow of the rugged hills which form here the northern boundary of the valley of the Dee, and has lovely views up and down the river, as well as of the wooded heights beyond, with the glorious outline of Loch-na-gar in the distance.

Few scenes could be more picturesque or more characteristic of Highland religious feeling than the old annual Sacrament Sunday on this spot,

generally the last Sunday in June, when the days
are long and bright. The people gathered early in
carts and other vehicles from distant parts of the
parish, and sat or stood in groups, conversing
quietly, on the green banks under the trees, before
the bell summoned to worship, and again at intervals throughout the day; a subdued hush over all,
as of reverence, mingling with the drowsy summer
stillness—a something not belonging to ordinary
Sabbaths, and to be felt rather than expressed.

Two long tables, covered with white linen, were
arranged across the centre of the church; and such
was the number of communicants that these were
generally cleared and refilled with fresh occupants
four or five times. Just under the pulpit was a
small table, also covered with a white cloth, on
which were placed the bread and wine. Presiding
at this, stood the clergyman who "served the
tables," as it was called, that is, gave a short
address before and after the administration of the
Sacrament; and round him were grouped the
officiating elders. The communicants entered and
left the tables to the strains of that grandest of
thanksgiving hymns—the 103rd Psalm, in the

beautiful Scottish metrical version, sung to the tune of " London New."

The services lasted five or six hours, and few of the people found them tedious, with the intervals of rest which their arrangement afforded ; touchingly solemn and impressive they always appeared to me.

For many years all this has been changed, and there are now spring and autumn Communions, with shortened services. No doubt the change is for the better in many ways, but there are some old folks who still look fondly back to the long summer Sabbath on the green hillside, where the mountains were round about us, as they encompassed Jerusalem of old on her solemn feast-day, and spoke the same message to our hearts, that the Lord is round about his people from henceforth even for ever.

It was after this change that the Queen was first present at the celebration of the Communion in Crathie, and she records in her *Journal* that she was "much impressed by the grand simplicity of the service."

It was not, however, until November, 1873, that the Sovereign first sat down among her Highland tenants and servants to partake with them of the

Lord's Supper. The Queen was seated in the manse pew, then included in " the tables," and my father, who for most of his life was an elder in Crathie Church, had the privilege of handing to Her Majesty the sacred elements for her first communion in the Scottish Church.

Many were found to cavil at the Queen's action in this matter, but it ever seemed to me only one among many instances of her wide sympathy and breadth of view, which could look beyond minor differences of ritual and ecclesiastical government, to the essentials of the Christian faith common to the English and Scottish Churches alike.

A handsome service of Communion plate, inscribed " Presented by H.M. Queen Victoria to the Church of Crathie, 1871," remains a lasting memorial of her interest in its ordinances and welfare.

Mr. Anderson, who for the first eighteen years of the Queen's residence at Balmoral was minister of Crathie, was a good, kind man, diligent in the service of his Master and people, and always at their call with spiritual or temporal counsel and comfort at any hour of the day or night. Though

not an eloquent man, his simple gospel preaching
was more appreciated by many of his congregation
than the more elaborate discourses which they often
heard.   In those days hotels on Deeside were
fewer, and means of communication less easy, so
in the autumn the minister practically kept open
house.   All were made welcome, and many were
the guests from far and near who claimed the ever-
ready hospitality of the Manse of Crathie.

One member of the congregation in those times
used to excite much interest and amusement among
strangers.   This was the minister's collie, who was
a regular attendant at church, following Mr. Anderson up the pulpit steps and quietly lying down at
the top.   He was always a most decorous, though
possibly somnolent listener, but he was also an
excellent timekeeper, for if the sermon was a few
minutes longer than usual Towser got up and
stretched himself, yawning audibly.   When the
Queen first came, Mr. Anderson feared she might
object to such an unorthodox addition to the congregation, and shut up Towser on Sunday.   Her
Majesty next day sent an equerry to the Manse to
inquire if anything had happened to the dog, as

she had a sketch of the interior of the church in which he appeared lying beside the pulpit, and if he were alive and well, she would like to see him in his old place. Greatly to Towser's delight he was thus by royal command restored to Church privileges.

He was a dog of strong Established Church principles, what would have been called "a rank Moderate" in old Disruption days. When Mr. Anderson officiated in Braemar as clergyman of the united parishes, Towser generally accompanied his master, and there also had his accustomed place. The doctor in Braemar was very fond of the dog, and occasionally took him home with him for a few days. One of these visits included a Sunday, and the doctor went, as was his custom, to the Free Church, followed to the door by Towser, who, having thus done his duty by his host, trotted off to the "auld kirk." The doctor was joked about the incident by some of his friends, and resolved that next time he would make sure of the dog's attendance, so provided himself with some favourite biscuits. Towser accompanied him to his pew, remained till the biscuits were finished, then slipped quietly out and set off at full speed for his accustomed place of worship, arriving just in time to gain admission before the doors were closed. The doctor was so annoyed at this second desertion that he made no further attempt to alter Towser's "Erastian" leanings.

In 1866 Mr. Anderson died, and was succeeded by Dr. Malcolm Taylor, a man of high culture and attainments, now Professor of Ecclesiastical History in Edinburgh University.

Large additions and improvements were made to the Manse at this time, and the stipend, which had been already augmented by the Queen in Mr. Anderson's case, was still further increased.

Dr. Taylor was succeeded in 1874 by Mr. Campbell, and during his incumbency a new church was erected on the old site, but this was long after the period to which these scattered recollections are confined. It is a handsome building, and more worthy of its prominent position in the country; but my heart clings to the "auld kirk," and, to adapt the words of Lady Nairne's touching song regarding her childhood's home, "there ne'er can be a new kirk (house) will seem sae fair to me."

When first I knew Crathie well, the Disruption was little more than a decade old, and for some years the small handful of Free Church people worshipped in my father's barn.   They had no settled minister, but in the summer clergymen from a distance and professors from the New Free Church colleges often conducted the services.   The wooden "louvre-windows" which ventilated and lighted the barn looked out upon the Mains garden, and enabled those outside to hear distinctly.   Many a good sermon, or selections therefrom, I have listened to, while enjoying the gooseberries and strawberries which grew below, and theology imbibed under such conditions ceased to be a dry subject to the youthful mind.   The old Scotch psalm tunes had a very pretty effect heard thus in the still summer evenings, notwithstanding that the voice of the precentor, a local shoemaker, was more remarkable for volume than music.

An enthusiastic Free Church friend used to dub my father "Obed-Edom" in those days, and say that a like blessing would rest upon his dwelling for thus sheltering the modern "Ark of God"!

After some years a site was obtained on the

Abergeldie property, near the Loch-na-gar distillery; a neat church was built, and the "ark"
removed to a more permanent and suitable resting-
place.

I remember well the laying of the foundation
stone of this building by Lord Dalhousie, a strong
supporter of the Free Church, who made a long
speech on the occasion.

He was a cold, unattractive man in manner, and
always appeared to me more of a political than a
religious Free Churchman. The Disruption coat
did not seem to fit naturally the well-known Fox-
Maule of the middle of last century. Any lack
of the ring of earnestness in his speech was made
up for by the eloquent sermon which followed from
Dr. Guthrie of Edinburgh, a man beloved and respected by all who knew him of whatever denomi-
nation. I shall never forget his striking figure, with
its grand, strongly marked old face and long white
hair, standing, head uncovered, under the blue sky,
with Nature's temple of woods and mountains all
around, and preaching the gospel message with
impassioned fervour.

I suppose this church was ultimately found in-

convenient and out of the way ; for recently a pretty
Church and Manse have been built near the centre
of the valley on a rising ground overhanging the
river, about a mile below Balmoral.   But this also
belongs to the many changes that have taken place
since my time.

CHAPTER VI

"HERE'S TO THEM THAT ARE GANE"

> "... No kinder breast
> Beats for the woes of the distrest,
> Bleeds for the wounds it cannot heal,
> Or yearns more o'er thy country's weal.
> Thy love embraces Britain o'er,
> And spreads and radiates with her shore."—Hogg.

> " Nowhere beats the heart so kindly
> As beneath the tartan plaid."—Aytoun.

The Queen among her Highland people—Appreciation of the Celtic nature—
Interest in the families of tenants and servants—Letters from the Queen—
John Grant—Johnnie and Annie Simpson—Willie Blair—Some other
Crathie worthies—Past and present—Fragment from Charles Kingsley.

The Queen was a frequent and, it is needless to
say, welcome visitor in the cottage homes of
Crathie.   Apart from her generous liberality—
sometimes, one is inclined to think, too lavish for
their good—the people really enjoyed talking to
her, always feeling sure of comprehension and sympathy, and not being oppressed with that nervous

sense of the greatness of their visitor which is apt
to affect some of the grades above them. The
Highlanders of the labouring class, both men and
women, fifty years ago had a natural dignity and
courtesy, combined with perfect self - possession,
in mixing with their superiors in station, which I
am sorry to say is fast dying out. It was very
marked in some of the old people I remember, and
induced the Queen, as well as many others, to say
that the Highlanders were born gentlemen and
ladies. The Celtic nature had always a great
charm for the Queen; she has herself said "Since
my great sorrow in 1861 I have found no natures
so sympathetic and so soothing as the Highlanders'."

The freedom of their homely speech interested
and amused her, for she well knew that no dis-
respect was meant, as when one woman would welcome her with the invitation "Come awa ben and
sit doon, Queen Victoria," or another "Is this you,
my Sovereign?" On one of her longer excursions
she once met and conversed with an old woman
who did not recognise her until the lady-in-waiting
told her that it was the Queen, when the old body

dropped her knitting, seized Her Majesty's hands, and exclaimed "What! the Queen! Happy and glorious, long to reign over us!"—a speech which gave great amusement and pleasure to her audience.

It often astonished our friends from the other side of the Border to hear, as I have frequently heard, the greatest lady in the land spoken of in homely fashion as "a fine body," or "a couthy cratur," but I fully believe these terms would have been heartily appreciated by the Queen had she heard them, for she valued the respect and love awarded her for her qualities as a woman, apart from her exalted rank.

To many of the children of her tenants and servants she stood godmother, and very numerous are the Victorias and Alberts reared in Crathie, whose education and start in life have been watched over and provided for by their royal sponsor. The large heart of the Queen, amid all the cares of State, could think of and sympathise with her humble Highland people, of whose joys and sorrows she always desired to be told. Writing the day before the arrival of H.R.H. the Duke of Edinburgh and his bride, her mind naturally full of her son and the new daughter she was so soon to welcome, she yet found time to say in a letter to my father dated March 6th, 1874 :—

The Queen is greatly grieved to hear of the continued indisposition of good Peter Farquharson,* and of the anxious state of poor Annie Symon, but she hopes and trusts both may yet improve.

Writing from Osborne on December 28th, 1869, she says :—

The Queen has (very tardily) to thank Dr. Robertson for his last letter. She is sorry he did not come through London on leaving Sandringham, so that she could have seen him. . . . The Queen hopes the dear people keep well, and relies on his giving them any assistance they may require. She was very sorry for the death of Morgan's brother Donald, and she fears it must be a heavy blow to the poor old mother. . . . She rejoices to hear that Dr. Taylor's administration of the Communion was satisfactory. The Queen cannot conclude without wishing Dr. Robertson and his family a very happy New Year. All the Highlanders here, she is glad to say, are well.

The judicious kindness of the Queen followed even the erring among her people. In one case

---

* A gamekeeper who had been many years on the Abergeldie property—a straightforward, excellent man, and a fine specimen of a Highlander.

a young man in her service gave himself up to drinking habits, was often forgiven, but eventually had to be dismissed. Another situation was found for him, but he could not keep it. He was then helped out to Australia and a fresh start given to him there. The Queen most wisely and kindly caused money to be sent to a relative in Australia, not to be given then, but to be kept for the poor fellow in case his besetting sin should bring him to poverty.

The churchyard of Crathie is a record of a Sovereign's appreciation of faithful service. Many are the monuments there erected by the Queen, and on each are some kindly words of appreciation and regret. One of the warmest tributes is paid on a mural tablet to the memory of John Grant, for nearly thirty years head keeper at Balmoral, but who is buried at Braemar. He was in many respects a typical Highlander both in appearance and character, tall and dark, with a striking, strongly marked face, the expression when at rest somewhat "dour" and hard, but lit up now and then by flashes of pawky humour. He had a quaint way of expressing himself, such as when, charac-

terising the shooting of a not very proficient sportsman with whom he had been out after deer, he said
"He has an ill fashion o' sheeting by them." A
term of Grant's, when deer-stalking and speaking
of the stags being on the alert and watchful, used
to amuse the Prince Consort, "Ye maun tak' care,
they're *jaylous* the day."

Grant was deeply attached to his royal mistress,
and consequently rather inclined himself to be
jealous in the more usual sense of the word, when,
as he thought, others were preferred before him.
This is a penalty often paid by the bestower and
receiver of a strong and exclusive devotion, but
none knew better than the Queen that it was a
leal-hearted, faithful servant to whom, though dead,
she yet testifies on the wall of Crathie churchyard.

Of more of the immediate retainers of the Queen
I need not speak, for nearly all have been im-
mortalised by her own pen. With one exception,
all her *earliest* servants have, like herself, passed
over to the Spirit Land. I believe, when our
present King and Queen came to their Highland home in 1901, only one — stalwart, honest
Donald Stewart, the head-keeper — remained to

welcome them of those who entered the royal service at Balmoral in 1848. But among the outer circle of tenants and employés many seem worthy of mention as characteristic of the time and place. They crowd around me as I write, vivid mental pictures from the land of shadows whither all have now passed, and I long for the pen of a Stevenson or a Barrie to clothe with life my " Memories and Portraits " of Crathie worthies.

About half a mile from Abergeldie is a nursery garden, intended to supplement the supplies of fruit and vegetables for the use of the castle, a garden divided into sections by hedgerows, as if an " eke " had been added on from the adjoining wood as occasion required. Presiding over this garden, in their quaintly named cottage of " Corbieha'," literally "Crow-hall," dwelt fifty years ago a charming old couple, Johnnie and Annie Simpson. Johnnie was an old bluejacket who had served under Nelson at the Battle of Copenhagen, for which he had a medal. He often went by the name of "Old 1801," and had, I think, been wounded in that or some other engagement. He was an infirm old man when I first remember him, but he got young again in fighting his battles over by the fireside or sitting in the garden, and many a yarn he spun of the great commander and the brave days of old. Over the fireplace " ben the hoose " were fixed Johnnie's old uniform, cutlass, and musket, which had seen good service in his country's cause. When our beloved Queen Alexandra, then Princess of Wales, first came to Abergeldie, Annie Simpson had serious thoughts of removing these memorials of Copenhagen, and was much relieved to find that the Princess was not sensitive on the subject, but much interested in seeing the weapons which had once been turned against her countrymen.

Annie was a picture of neatness in her plain winsey, or print gown, according to the season, a little tartan shawl pinned over her shoulders, a spotless apron, and big "mutch," under which beamed the kindliest of faces, frequently puckered up into innumerable wrinkles by a hearty laugh, which latterly, alas! often ended in a terrible fit of coughing, for poor old Annie's chest was much oppressed by what she called "a closin'." The bright old woman was a great favourite with the Royal Family, and many were the gifts and com-

JOHN AND ANNIE SIMPSON

To face p. 120

forts she received from them, of which she was
not a little proud.   I remember being permitted by
Annie to sit—for a few minutes only—in a very
cosy armchair just given to her by the Princess of
Wales, who in thoughtful kindness towards her poor
neighbours and dependants is a worthy successor
to Her late Majesty.   Sometimes on going into her
cottage while the Court was at Balmoral, we would
be greeted with uplifted hands and " I'm ower
prood to shak hands wi' ye the day, I've hed the
Queen."   Then fearing (very needlessly) that we
might be offended, we would be "clapped" (patted)
on the shoulders and coaxingly told, "Oh, niver
heed auld Annie, I'm jist a feel (foolish) body."

When we paid her a visit we had always to walk
round the garden and "get a floore," as she expressed it, and for every plant that grew at
Corbieha' Annie had a name.   These were not
always to be found in a botanical book, but no
matter—what she did not know she constructed,
and very clever she was at it.   I have often wished
I had compiled a floral dictionary from Annie, but
only one name remains in my memory, and by it a
certain double yellow blossoming shrub is always

known in my garden. Its right name I forget, but Annie's, spelt phonetically, sounded like "Laradiddamy"!

Annie survived Johnnie for several years, but for many a day now they have lain side by side in Crathie churchyard.

Among the notabilities of the parish none deserves a higher place than Willie Blair, the Queen's fiddler, as he was called, an indispensable guest at every festive gathering. Willie well merited the title often bestowed on him of the Neil Gow of Deeside, for not only was he an admirable interpreter of that great master of Scottish reels, but he was no mean composer himself. "The Brig of Crathie" and "Miss Anderson's Strathspey," both of his composition, are admirable dancing tunes. Willie was a bit of a wag in a kindly, cynical fashion, and it was amusing to watch his face as he played. Quite at home with his instrument, he was free to notice what went on around him, and was a keen critic of the dancers. On one occasion he delighted a lady by assuring her that there was not a dancer on the floor like her husband; this was undoubtedly true, though not in the sense accepted by her, for the gentleman in question was equally ignorant of time and tune.

So stirring were the strains of Willie's fiddle that few could sit still when his bow was at work. The fame of his Scottish music reached beyond the upper valley of the Dee, for once he went on tour to Ireland with Julian Adams' band. When asked how the Dublin people liked his music, his reply was, " Raal weel, they jist pattered me back ilka time"; "encore" was not in Willie's vocabulary. Willie had a formidable rival on the other side of the Grampians with whom he met sometimes for a musical duel. I think the battle was generally admitted to be a drawn one, and Willie was too fair-minded not to allow the Perthshire man a qualified measure of approval. He used to say, "Ay! he *can play*, but he hasna jist the stott o't." By this he meant the special marking of the time, which is a most essential feature in reel playing.

So much was Willie in social request that over-conviviality was apt to follow. When this occurred he always made his way at once to the Manse to take what is called in Scotland "the first word o' flytin'," for the minister had often warned Willie

against over-indulgence on festive occasions when
the whisky bottle circulated freely. Asking to see
the minister, he would say, " I've been ower at a
dance at the Inver, Mr. Anderson, and I jist cam on
my wye hame that ye micht see me, in case ye sud
hear I wis waur nor I am."

Willie lived to be over ninety and fiddled almost
to the last.

In a pretty cottage on the bank which overhangs
the Dee near the chain bridge lived, at the time of
which I write, the Excise officer, or gauger, as he was
called, a functionary rendered necessary by the
prevalence of smuggling in the early half of last
century, and afterwards by the near neighbourhood
of the Loch-na-gar distillery.

Mr. and Mrs. Rose were an elderly couple when
I knew them, superior in education and class to
most of their neighbours—" the natives " Mrs. Rose
used to call them—kind and good to the core, but
full of quaint, amusing ways, which only endeared
them the more to their friends. Mrs. Rose was a
woman of commanding aspect, especially when sur-
mounted, as she generally was when she took her
walks abroad, by a very big bonnet and long lace

WILLIE BLAIR

To face p. 124

veil over her face, and her appearance won for her
the sobriquet of "The Major." Mr. Rose was a
meek man, proud of having won for his wife the
widow of a captain of Dragoons, for Mrs. Rose had
followed the colours before she entered the civil
service, and the halo of "the long sword, saddle,
bridle," etc., still surrounded her. The deceased
officer was much quoted by both the new partners,
and his regimental buttons worn and exhibited with
pride and pleasure by his successor!

It seems to me as if my little group of Crathie
folk would be incomplete without Mary McHardy,
my father's old housekeeper at the Mains, for she
was a Crathie woman by birth, as well as latterly by
residence, and a perfect type of a now extinct class,
the trusty, free-spoken Scotch family servant of old
days.

Mary had been in my father's service in various
capacities for five-and-twenty years, when in 1854
he took the farm of Mains of Abergeldie, and
she left our home at Indego to become housekeeper at the Mains. There she served him
faithfully for another term of more than twenty
years, and was "faithful unto death," for she did

not long survive her retirement to a cottage at
Crathinaird.

In 1854 the Mains was little more than an ordinary farmhouse, but at various times subsequently it
was added to by the Queen, and used during her
autumn stay at Balmoral as a residence for the wife
and family of one of the gentlemen connected with
the Court—Sir Charles Phipps, Sir Thomas Bid-
dulph, etc. At all other times it was a second
home to us, and my father generally spent part of
every week there, often accompanied by some
member of his family. We loved the picnic sort
of life, and Mary always made us welcome when
alone, but visitors in any number, especially some
people, she strongly objected to, as she "couldna
thole the scutter o' fine cooking," as she phrased it ;
it was therefore quite a diplomatic mission, often
passed on by one member of the family to another,
to warn Mary of the advent of certain guests.
She was characterised by great plainness of speech,
and had a forcible vocabulary at times ; her bark
was much worse than her bite however, and she
did her best eventually to make everybody comfortable. She always styled my father Him and Him-

sel' with a capital H, and, truth to tell, I think he
was at heart sometimes a little afraid of her; but he
knew her worth and value as well as Mary knew
her power. She often scolded my sister and me,
but woe be to anyone else who dared to say a
word against us! My brother—"her laddie," as
she used to call him—could do no wrong. Mary
was inclined to jeer at the brevet rank of "Mrs."
bestowed upon her by the autumn tenants of the
Mains, it not being usual in Scotland in her
early days to give the title even to upper servants,
unless married. "I'm Mistress McHardy," she
would say, with emphasis, "when the gran' folks
are here, but I'm jist plain Mary again noo." Mary
had a great respect for the Queen's powers of
observation. Her Majesty always personally in-
spected any alterations made at the Mains, and
Mary used to say, "I maun hae iverything snod
(tidy) or the Queen come, for naething escapes her
een." Dear old Mary! I can see her now enjoying
her cutty pipe by the fire in the kitchen, for she
was one of the few women-smokers left in our
part of the country in my young days. "She
couldna dee wintin' her smoke," she used to say,

and she could get no more acceptable gift than a packet of the strong-flavoured brown twist to be got at Symon, "the mairchant's." Mary was an excellent dairy and poultry woman, and her "beasts"—the term included the fowls—must be properly attended to whatever happened to the humans.

Many others come up before me as I write, some best known by their nicknames, such as the "Professor," the "Shirra," or the "Minister of the Camlet." In fact they so rarely got any other appellation that one was apt to forget they possessed any. The "Professor" dwelt on the north side of the river and was much given to spouting poetry, but his elocutionary efforts were not so successful as his stuffing of birds and stags' heads, at which he was quite an adept.

The "Minister of the Camlet" was of sanctified mien and semiclerical get-up, with a furtive way of looking beneath his eyebrows, which did not inspire confidence when he took up the rôle of a prophet. He was fond of dwelling upon "the mark of the beast," and allocated it with considerable freedom; while upon the "Battle of

Armageddon," to be fought, he said, somewhere in the valley of the Dee between Crathie and Braemar, he used to wax fiercely eloquent.

The "Shirra" was a well-known figure in the Abergeldie neighbourhood; lithe and active, he gained his name, I believe, because often called upon to act as umpire in competitions and to settle disputes of various kinds among his neighbours. He was the *Jhuth-Singh* of Crathie, and when he prefaced a statement by the words, "This is no a lee I'm telling ye," the hearer felt he was in for a very tall story indeed!

Many might be added to the little group I have faintly sketched, for there was more individuality fifty years ago than exists now. Increased education and facilities for travelling have caused a growing assimilation of dress, manners, and customs all over the kingdom, and though the gain may be great, modern progress has to a great extent quenched originality.

These old folks belong to a past Crathie, and such are the changes which years bring that when I revisit Deeside I feel a stranger in the land I once knew so well. The dear old mountains and

K

woods and rushing river remain, but those who live and walk among them are a new generation. Therefore in these pages I have loved to shut my eyes upon modern Crathie, and people the beautiful valley with the familiar forms and faces who made its life in bygone days.

> " They drift away.   Ah, God ! they drift for ever.
>   I watch the stream sweep onward to the sea,
> Like some old battered buoy upon a roaring river,
>   Round whom the tide-waifs hang—then drift to sea.
> I watch them drift—the old familiar faces,
>   Who fished and rode with me, by stream and wold,
> Till ghosts, not men, fill old beloved places,
>   And, ah ! the land is rank with churchyard mould.
>
>   .   .   .   .   .   .
>
> Yet overhead the boundless arch of heaven
>   Still fades to-night, still blazes into day.
>
>   .   .   .   .   .
>
> Ah, God !   My God ! Thou wilt not drift away."
>
> C. KINGSLEY.

THE END

INDEX

Ministers at Balmoral, 49
" Monkey," 33
Murray, Lord and Lady James, 85

Palmerston, Lord, 51
Princess Royal. *See* Frederick, Empress
" Professor," the, 128

Robertson, Dr., 15 ; appointed Commissioner, 31 ; letters from Queen Victoria, 44, 62–5, 69, 102, 116 ; inscriptions of books from Her Majesty, 61 ; visit of sympathy, 64 ; resigns Commissionership to the Queen, 69 ; death of, 70
Rose, Mr. and Mrs., 124
Ross, Mrs. Horatio, 26
Russell, Earl, 50

Sacrament Sunday, 103
" Shirra," the, 129
Simpson, Johnnie and Annie, 119
Smith, William, 38

Stanley, Lady Augusta. *See* Bruce

Taylor, Dr. Malcolm, 57, 109
Theed, Mr., 59
Towser, the collie, 108

Victoria, H.M. Queen : goes to Balmoral, 29, 30 ; in Crathie Church, 33, 99, 106 ; her gracious motherliness, 41 ; letters, 44, 62–5, 72, 102, 116 ; manages Balmoral, 60 ; rents Ballochbuie Forest, 62 ; sense of humour, 66 ; her sympathy, 71 ; letter to the author, 72 ; leases Abergeldie, 75 ; tribute to Dr. McLeod, 101 ; presents Communion plate to Crathie Church, 106 ; visits the cottagers, 113 ; acts as godmother, 115 ; instances of generosity, 117

Wages of servants, 6
Wales, H.R.H. Prince of. *See* Edward VII.

Ingram Content Group UK Ltd.
Milton Keynes UK
UKHW020647150523
421757UK00007B/419